The Encyclopedia of

KEYBOARD COLOR PICTURE CHORDS

Amsco Publications
A Part of **The Music Sales Group**
New York/London/Paris/Sydney/Copenhagen/Berlin/Tokyo/Madrid

Photography: Randall Wallace
Illustration: Matthew Staples
Project editor: Felipe Orozco
Interior design and layout: Len Vogler

Order No. AM 982157
International Standard Book Number: 0.8256.3376.1

Exclusive Distributors:
Music Sales Corporation
257 Park Avenue South, New York, NY 10010 USA
Music Sales Limited
8/9 Frith Street, London W1D 3JB England
Music Sales Pty. Limited
120 Rothschild Street, Rosebery, Sydney, NSW 2018, Australia

Printed in the United States of America by
Vicks Lithograph and Printing Corporation

Table of Contents

How to Use This Book

There's a lot more to playing piano than just banging out a bunch of chords and trying to make it sound like a sonata or concerto—but then again, we're not all Mozart, are we? Nevertheless, the idea of playing for the sheer enjoyment of it is very appealing to most of us. Hence, this book. Playing chords on a piano is a great way to accompany yourself. You simply read the chord names on the sheet music, play the chords, and sing along. Although it might take a little practice to move from one chord to another, eventually you will be able to play and sing along with all your favorite melodies. And with the addition of some bass notes and chord inversions, you will be sounding like a pro in no time. This book is divided into twelve parts—one part for every key. These parts are arranged *chromatically*—one half-step at a time—from the key of C up to the key of B. Each key has a tab with a different color, this makes it easy to find the chords you need right away. There are two sections for each key: The first section contains chords that are made up of three or four notes and can be played with one hand. These are chords such as major, minor, augmented, diminished, and so on. The second section is made up of chords with five or more notes and are usually played with two hands. These chords are extended chords, such as 9, major9#11, major13, and so on. For each chord there are four elements—the chord name, photo, keyboard diagram, and the notes of the chord or *chord spelling.*

The *chord name* is just that, the name of the chord. There are different names and symbols for chords, but the names used in this book are fairly common and are what you are likely to see in sheet music and music books (for alternate chord names see page 10).

The *photo* shows you where to put your hands on the keyboard. Most of the photos use hand positions that were chosen with the beginning player in mind—basically these fingerings are the easiest and most comfortable in most situations. You will notice that the hands are not centered on every photograph, this is to show how the hand moves in relationship to the *tonic* or *root note* and to provide you with a better viewpoint when playing these chords on your piano or electronic keyboard (your keyboard doesn't move—your hands do).

The *keyboard diagram,* under the photo, shows which keys are used to make up the chord. The root of each chord is shown with a circle around it. Finally, the *notes of the chord* are shown directly below or above each key. These are the notes that make up the chord. Sometimes you will see note names that may not be familiar to you, like Cb or B#. Don't panic, these are enharmonic spellings (explained on page 254).

Alternate Chord Names

This chord encyclopedia uses a standard chord-naming approach, but when playing from sheet music or using other music books, you will find alternative chord names or symbols. Below is a chart by which you can cross reference alternative names and symbols with the ones used in this book.

Chord Name	Alternate Name or Symbol
major	M; Maj
minor	m; min; -
6	Maj6; M6
minor6	min6; -6
6/9	6(add9); Maj6(add9); M6(add9)
major7	M7; Maj7; Δ 7; Δ
7	dominant seventh; dom
7♭5	7(♭5); 7(-5)
7♯5	+7; 7(+5); aug7
minor7	m7; min7; -7
minor (major7)	m(M7); min(Maj7); m(+7); -(M7); min(addM7)
minor7♭5	∅7; ½dim; ½dim7; m7(♭5); m7(-5)
°7	°; dim; dim7
9	7(add9)
9♭5	9(♭5); 9(-5)
9♯5	+9; 9(+5); aug9
major9	M9; Δ 9; Maj7(add9); M7(add9)
7♭9	7(♭9); 7(add♭9); 7-9; -9
minor11	m11; min11
♯11	(+11); Δ (+11); M7(+11); Δ (♯11); M7(♯11)
13	7(add13); 7(add6)
major13	M13; Δ (add13); Maj7(add13); M7(add13); M7(add6)
minor13	m13; -13; min7(add13); m7(add13); -7 (add 13);
sus4	(sus4)
augmented	aug; (♯5); +5

C chords

C major

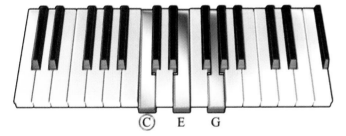

Ⓒ   E   G

C/E *(first inversion)*

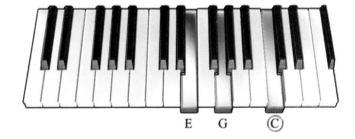

E   G   Ⓒ

C/G *(second inversion)*

G   Ⓒ   E

C augmented

G#

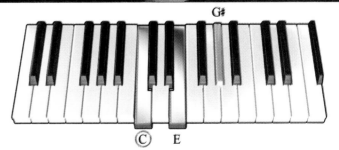

Ⓒ   E

C augmented *(first inversion)*

G#

E   Ⓒ

C augmented *(second inversion)*

G#

Ⓒ   E

Csus4

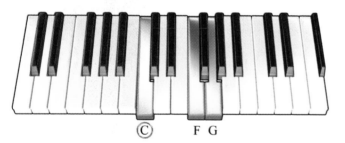

Ⓒ   F   G

Csus4 *(first inversion)*

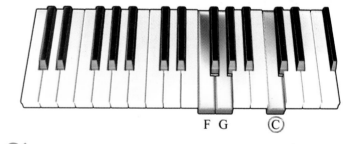

F   G   Ⓒ

Csus4 *(second inversion)*

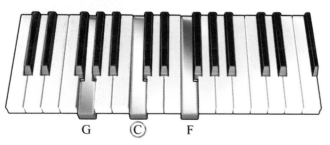

G   Ⓒ   F

C6

Ⓒ   E   G A

C6 (first inversion)

E   G A   Ⓒ

C6 (second inversion)

G A Ⓒ   E

C6 (third inversion)

A Ⓒ   E   G

C7

B♭

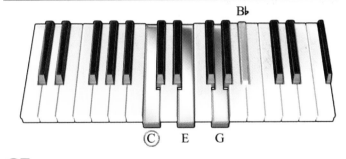

Ⓒ   E   G

C7 (first inversion)

B♭

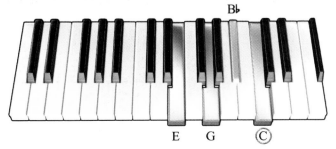

E   G   Ⓒ

C7 (second inversion)

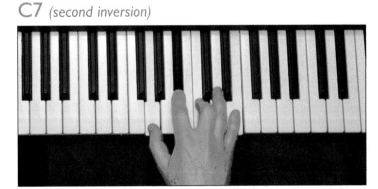

B♭

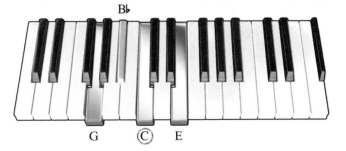

G   Ⓒ E

C7 *(third inversion)*

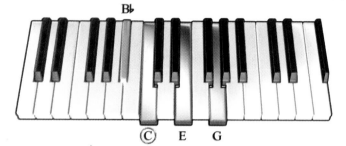

B♭

Ⓒ   E   G

C°7

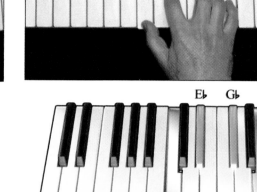

E♭   G♭

Ⓒ   B♭♭

C°7 *(first inversion)*

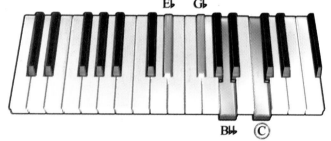

E♭   G♭

B♭♭   Ⓒ

C°7 *(second inversion)*

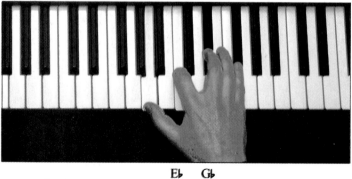

G♭   E♭

B♭♭   Ⓒ

C°7 *(third inversion)*

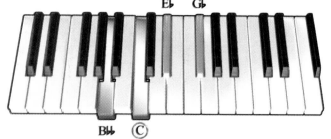

E♭   G♭

B♭♭   Ⓒ

C major7

Ⓒ   E   G   B

C

C major7 *(first inversion)*

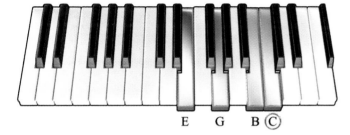

E G B Ⓒ

C major7 *(second inversion)*

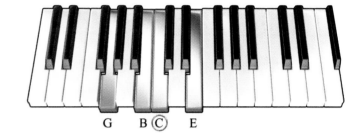

G B Ⓒ E

C major7 *(third inversion)*

B Ⓒ E G

C minor

E♭

Ⓒ G

C minor *(first inversion)*

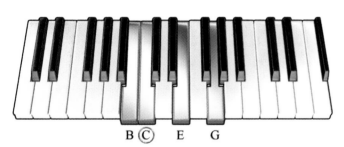

E♭

G Ⓒ

C minor *(second inversion)*

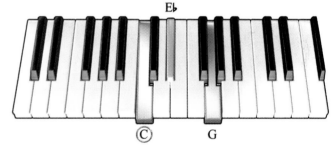

E♭

G Ⓒ

C minor6

E♭

Ⓒ   G A

C minor6 *(first inversion)*

E♭

G A Ⓒ

C minor6 *(second inversion)*

E♭

G A Ⓒ

C minor6 *(third inversion)*

E♭

A Ⓒ   G

C minor7

E♭   B♭

Ⓒ   G

C minor7 *(first inversion)*

E♭   B♭

G   Ⓒ

C minor7 *(second inversion)*

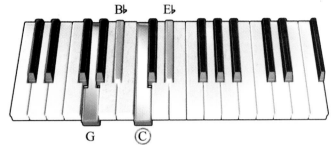

B♭ E♭
G Ⓒ

C minor7 *(third inversion)*

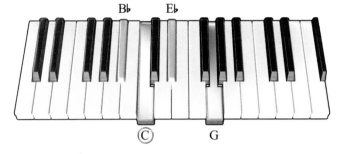

B♭ E♭
Ⓒ G

C minor7♭5

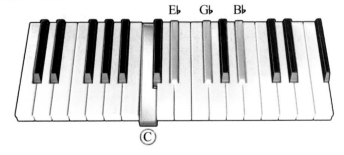

E♭ G♭ B♭
Ⓒ

C minor7♭5 *(first inversion)*

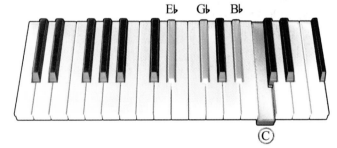

E♭ G♭ B♭
Ⓒ

C minor7♭5 *(second inversion)*

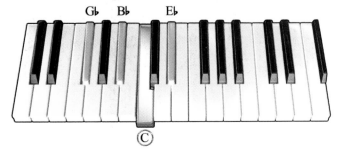

G♭ B♭ E♭
Ⓒ

C minor7♭5 *(third inversion)*

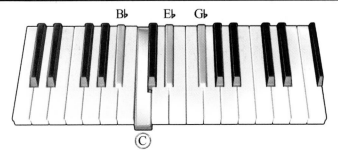

B♭ E♭ G♭
Ⓒ

C minor (major7)

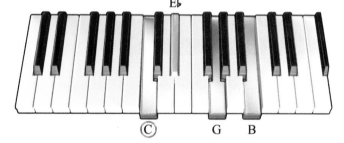

Eb

Ⓒ   G   B

C minor (major7) *(first inversion)*

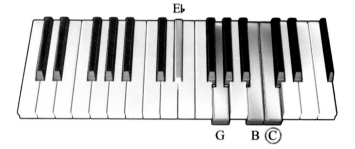

Eb

G   B Ⓒ

C minor (major7) *(second inversion)*

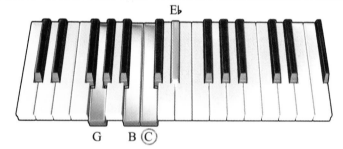

Eb

G   B Ⓒ

C minor (major7) *(third inversion)*

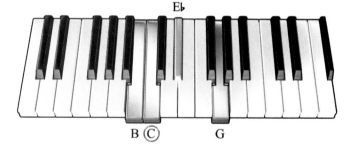

Eb

B Ⓒ   G

C chords
using both hands

C7♭9

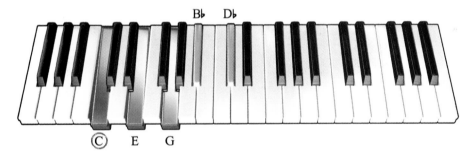

B♭   D♭

Ⓒ   E   G

C7♯9

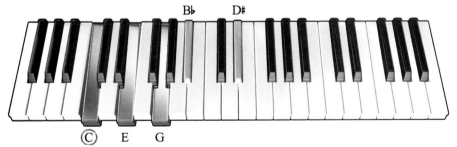

B♭   D♯

Ⓒ   E   G

C9

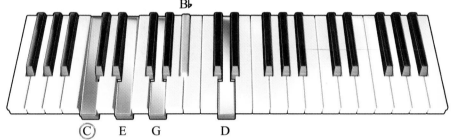

C9sus4

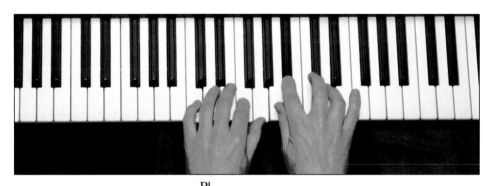

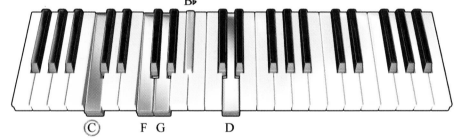

C9♭5

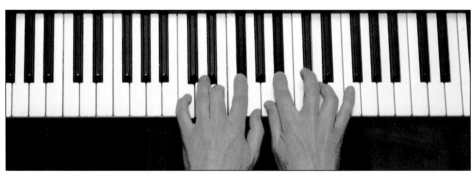

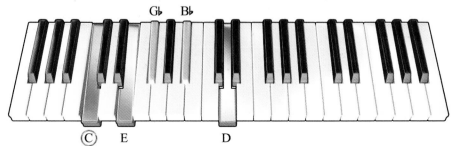

C9#5

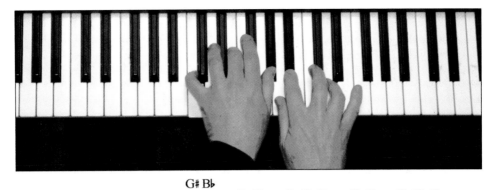

G# Bb

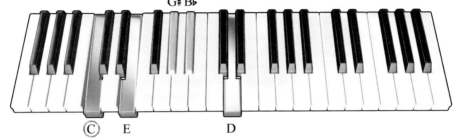

Ⓒ   E   D

C9#11

Bb   F#

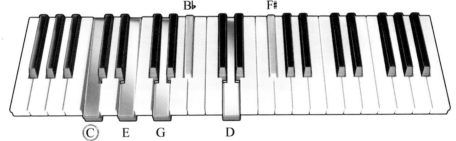

Ⓒ   E   G   D

C13

Bb

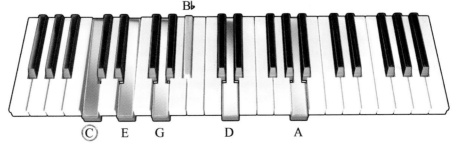

Ⓒ   E   G   D   A

C13sus4

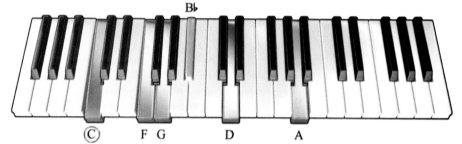

Bb

C F G D A

C13b5

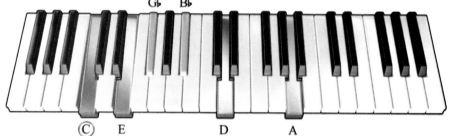

Gb Bb

C E D A

C13#5

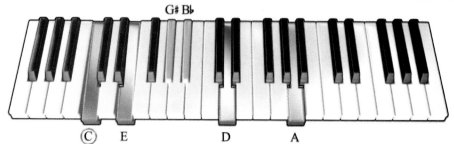

G# Bb

C E D A

C

C13♭9

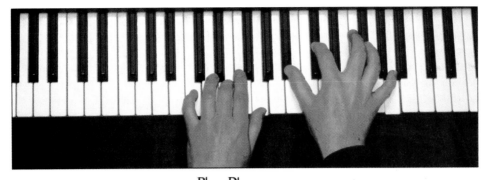

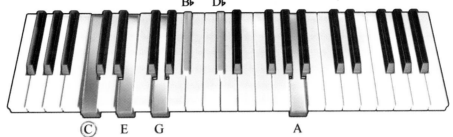

B♭ D♭

© E G A

C13♯9

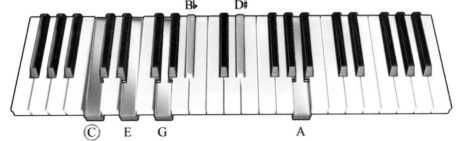

B♭ D♯

© E G A

C13♭5♭9

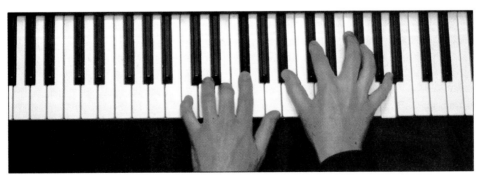

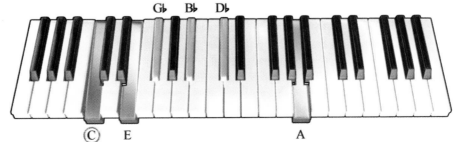

G♭ B♭ D♭

© E A

C13b5#9

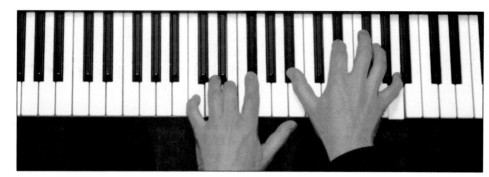

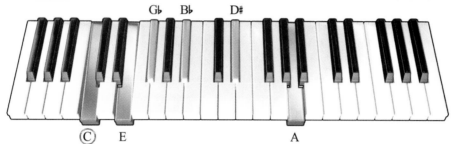

C13#5b9

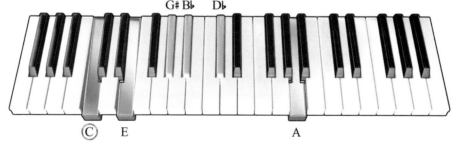

C13#5#9

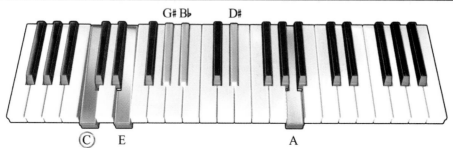

C 6/9

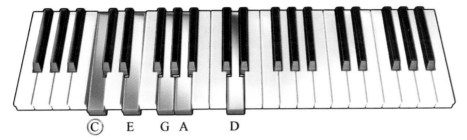

Ⓒ E G A D

C major9

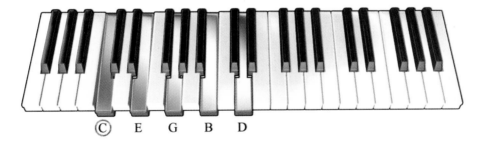

Ⓒ E G B D

C major9#11

F#

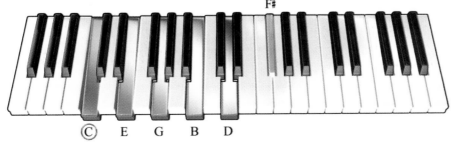

Ⓒ E G B D

C major13

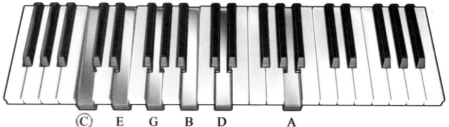

Ⓒ   E   G   B   D   A

C major13♭5

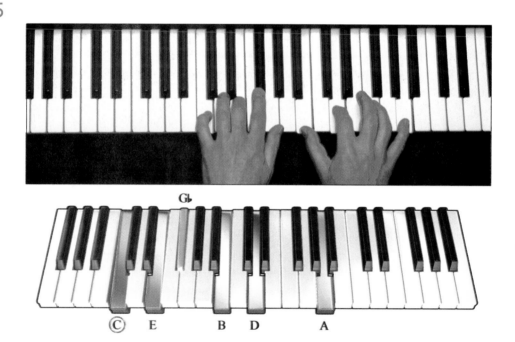

G♭

Ⓒ   E   B   D   A

C major13♯5

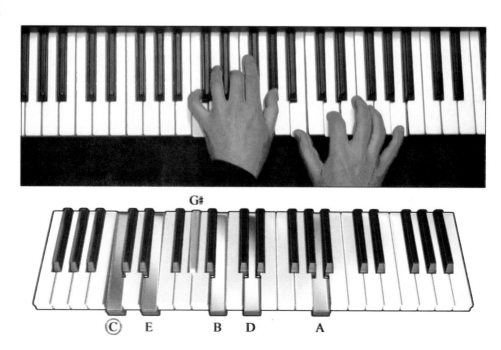

G♯

Ⓒ   E   B   D   A

C major13♭9

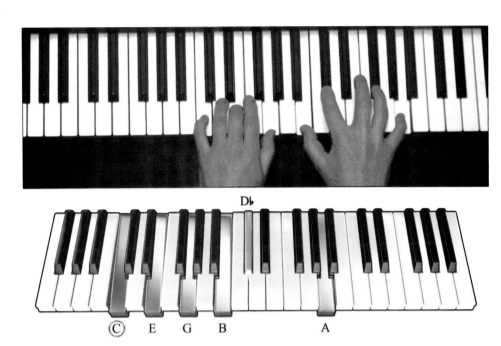

D♭

© E G B A

C major13♯9

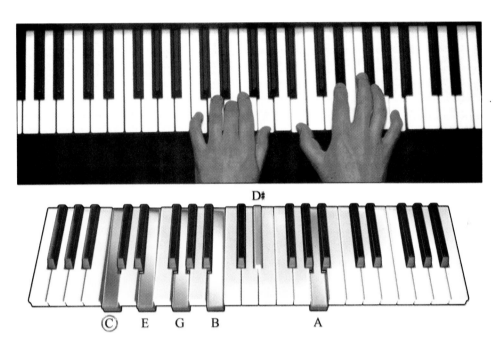

D♯

© E G B A

C major13♭5♭9

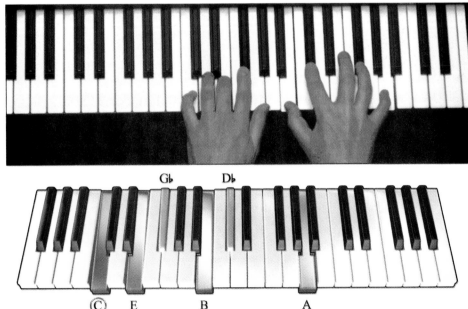

G♭ D♭

© E B A

C major13♭5♯9

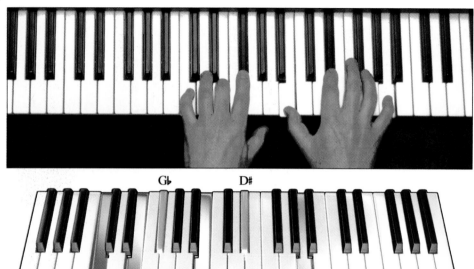

G♭   D♯

Ⓒ   E   B   A

C major13♯5♭9

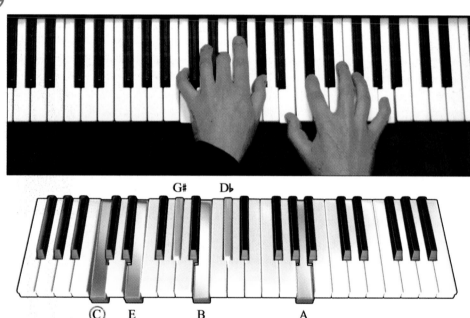

G♯   D♭

Ⓒ   E   B   A

C major13♯5♯9

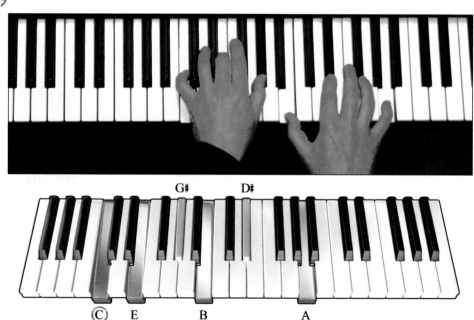

G♯   D♯

Ⓒ   E   B   A

C minor7♭9

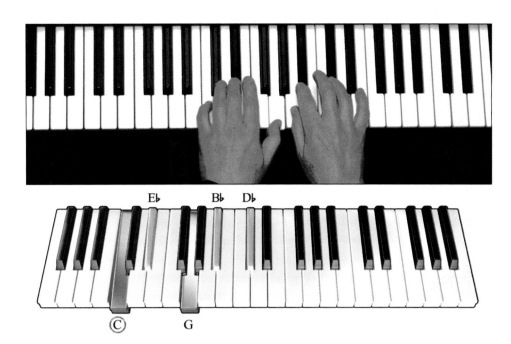

C minor9

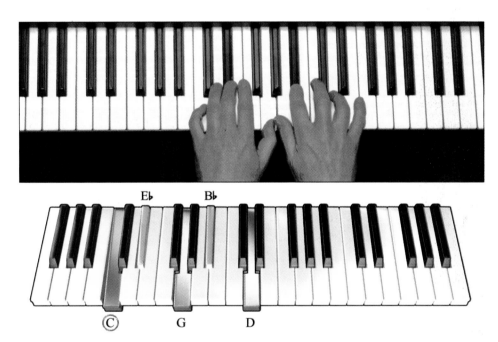

C minor11

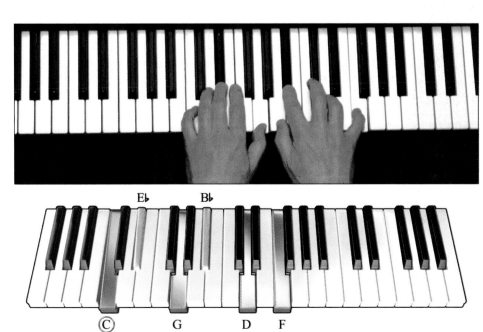

C minor13

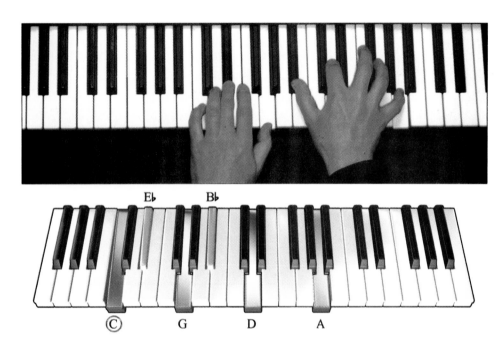

C minor9 (major7)

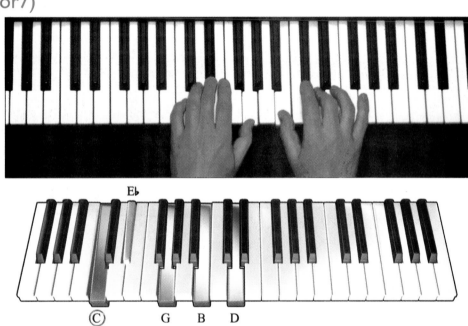

D♭ chords

D♭ major

(D♭)   A♭

F

D♭/F (first inversion)

A♭   (D♭)

F

D♭/A♭ (second inversion)

A♭   (D♭)

F

D♭ augmented

(D♭)

F   A

D♭ augmented *(first inversion)*

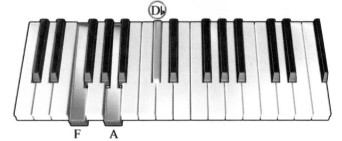

F   A

D♭ augmented *(second inversion)*

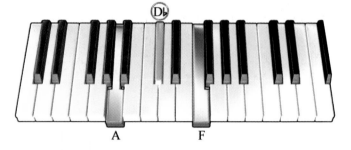

A   F

D♭sus4

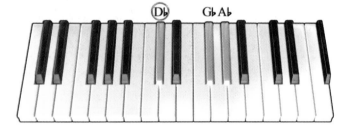

D♭   G♭ A♭

D♭sus4 *(first inversion)*

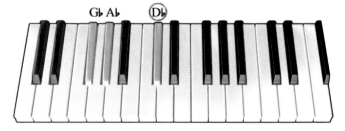

G♭ A♭   D♭

D♭sus4 *(second inversion)*

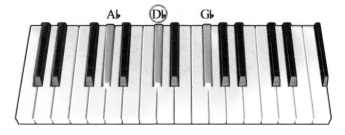

A♭   D♭   G♭

D♭6

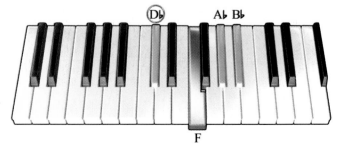

D♭   A♭ B♭

F

D♭

D♭6 *(first inversion)*

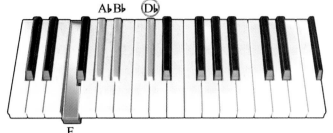

A♭ B♭ (D♭)

F

D♭6 *(second inversion)*

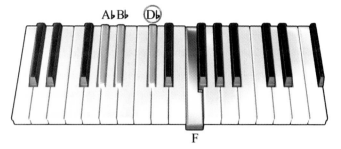

A♭ B♭ (D♭)

F

D♭6 *(third inversion)*

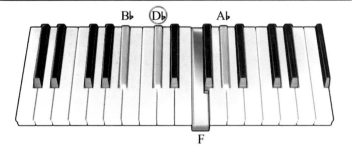

B♭ (D♭)   A♭

F

D♭7

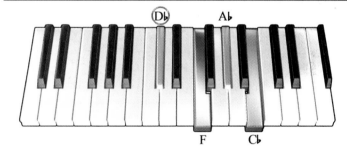

(D♭)   A♭

F   C♭

D♭7 *(first inversion)*

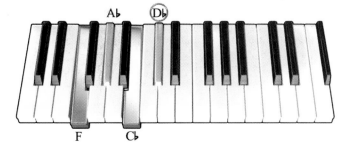

A♭ (D♭)

F   C♭

D♭7 *(second inversion)*

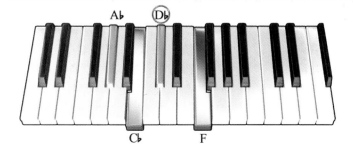

A♭ (D♭)

C♭   F

D♭7 (third inversion)

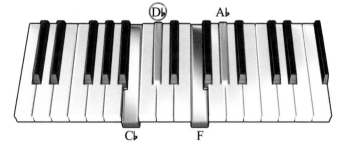

D♭ · A♭ · C♭ · F

D♭°7

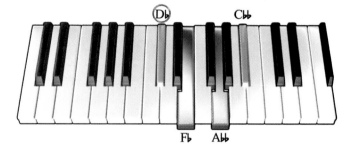

D♭ · C♭♭ · F♭ · A♭♭

D♭°7 (first inversion)

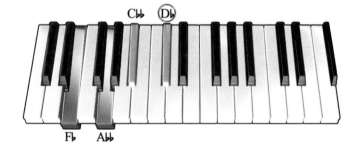

C♭♭ · D♭ · F♭ · A♭♭

D♭°7 (second inversion)

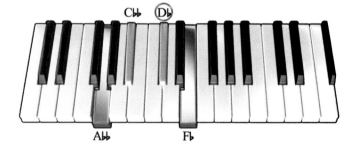

C♭♭ · D♭ · A♭♭ · F♭

D♭°7 (third inversion)

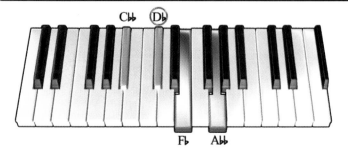

C♭♭ · D♭ · F♭ · A♭♭

D♭ major7

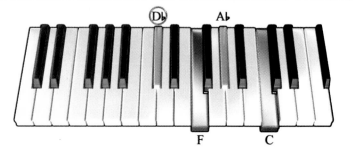

D♭ · A♭ · F · C

D♭ major7 *(first inversion)*

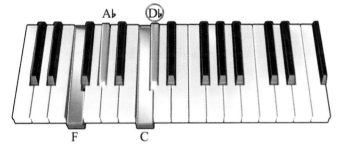

A♭ (D♭)

F   C

D♭ major7 *(second inversion)*

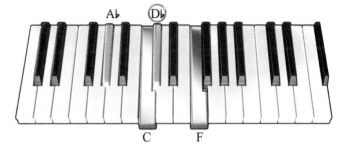

A♭ (D♭)

C   F

D♭ major7 *(third inversion)*

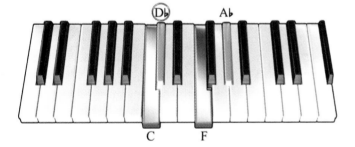

(D♭)   A♭

C   F

D♭ minor

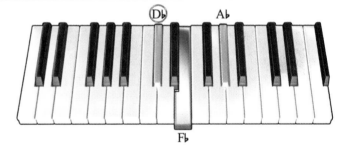

(D♭)   A♭

F♭

D♭ minor *(first inversion)*

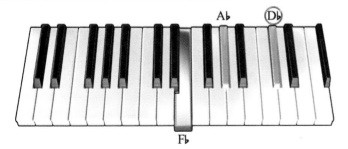

A♭   (D♭)

F♭

D♭ minor *(second inversion)*

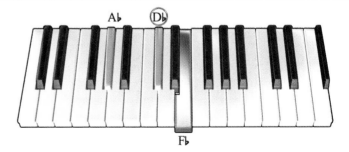

A♭   (D♭)

F♭

D♭

Db minor6

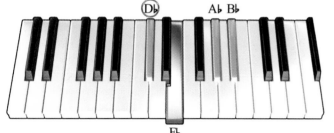

Db minor6 *(first inversion)*

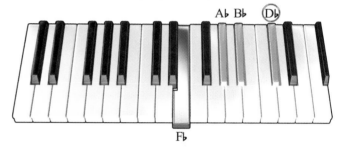

Db minor6 *(second inversion)*

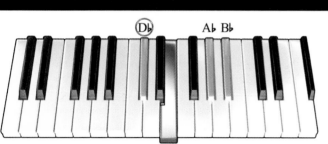

Db minor6 *(third inversion)*

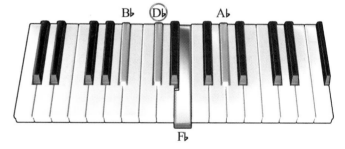

Db minor7

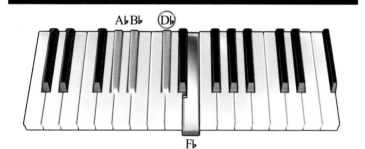

Db minor7 *(first inversion)*

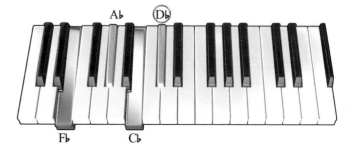

Db minor7 (second inversion)

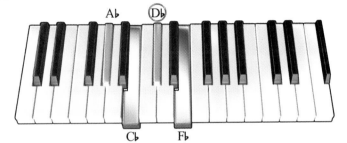

Ab (Db)

Cb Fb

Db minor7 (third inversion)

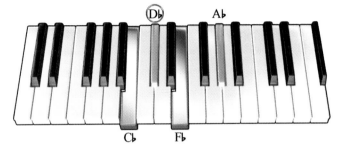

(Db) Ab

Cb Fb

Db minor7b5

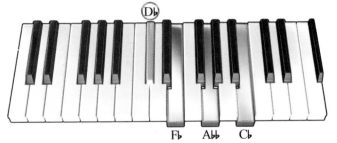

(Db)

Fb Abb Cb

Db minor7b5 (first inversion)

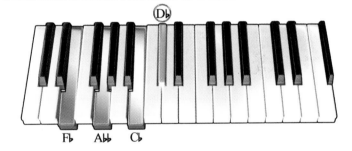

(Db)

Fb Abb Cb

Db minor7b5 (second inversion)

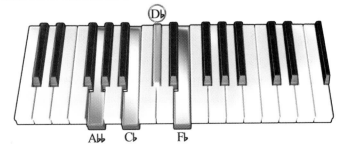

(Db)

Abb Cb Fb

Db minor7b5 (third inversion)

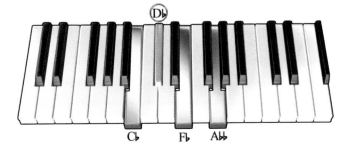

(Db)

Cb Fb Abb

Db

Db minor (major7)

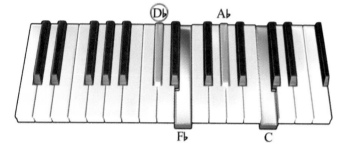

Db minor (major7) *(first inversion)*

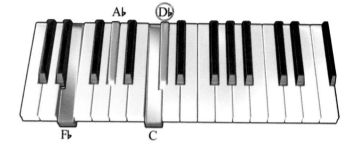

Db minor (major7) *(second inversion)*

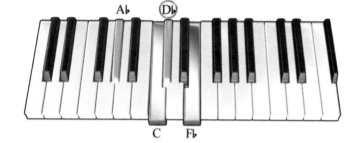

Db minor (major7) *(third inversion)*

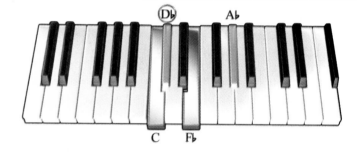

D♭ chords
using both hands

D♭7♭9

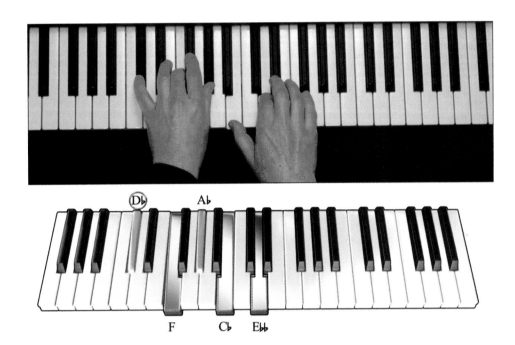

D♭7♯9

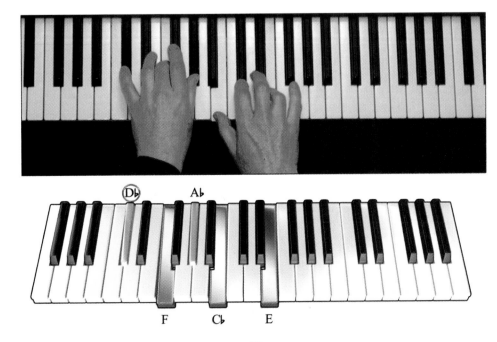

D♭9

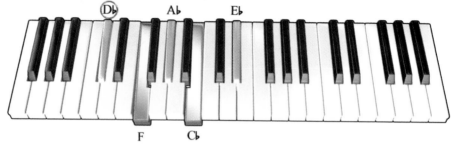

D♭9sus4

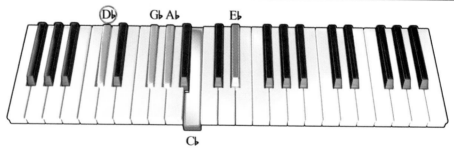

D♭9♭5

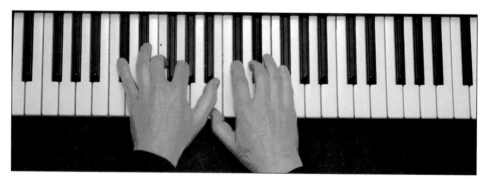

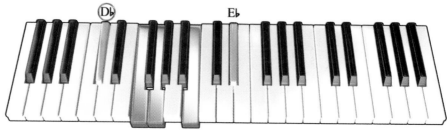

Db

Db9#5

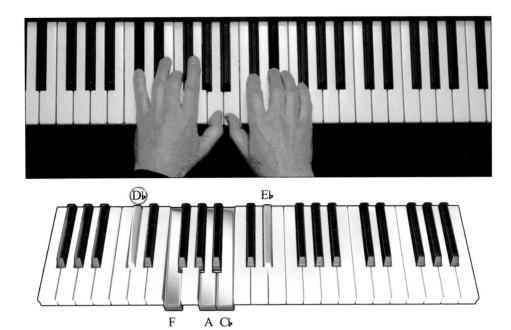

Db   Eb

F   A Cb

Db9#11

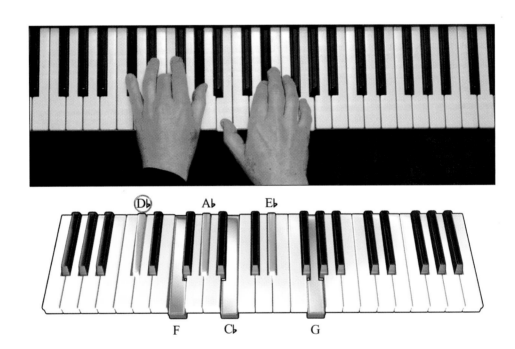

Db   Ab   Eb

F   Cb   G

Db13

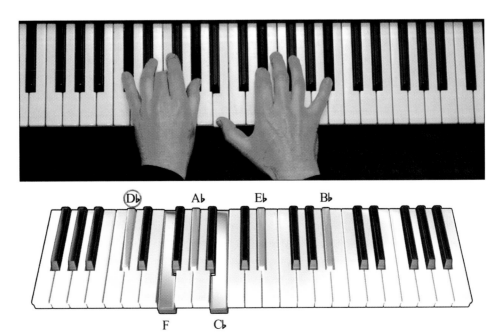

Db   Ab   Eb   Bb

F   Cb

D♭13sus4

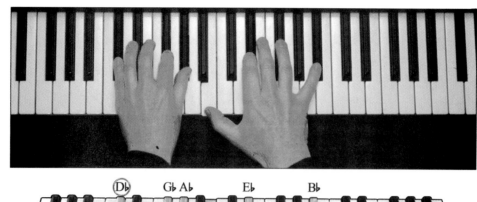

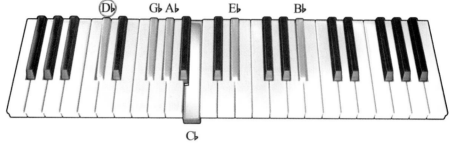

D♭13♭5

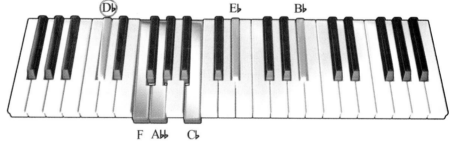

D♭13#5

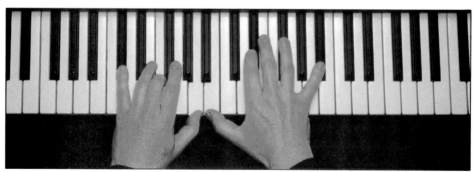

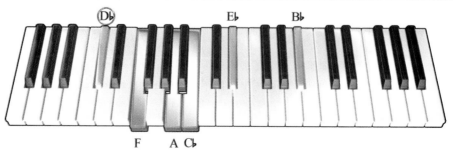

Db13b9

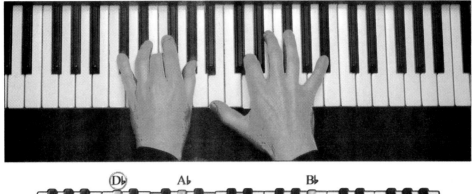

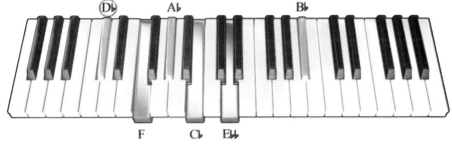

Db Ab Bb

F Cb Ebb

Db13#9

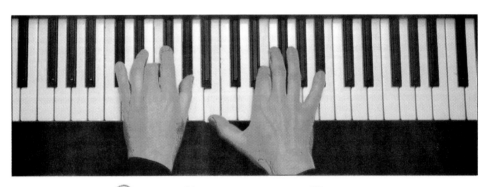

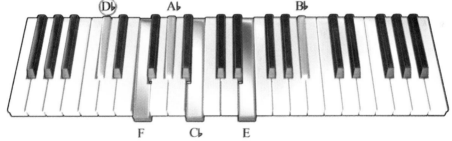

Db Ab Bb

F Cb E

Db13b5b9

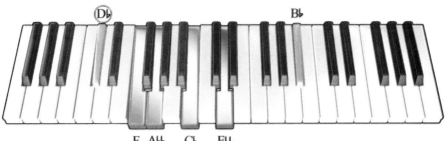

Db Bb

F Abb Cb Ebb

Db13b5#9

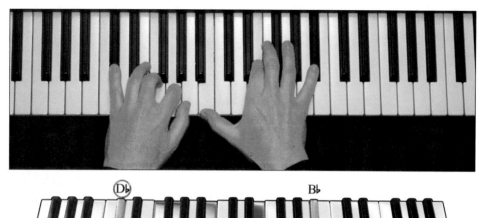

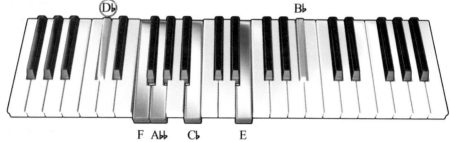

F Abb Cb E

Db13#5b9

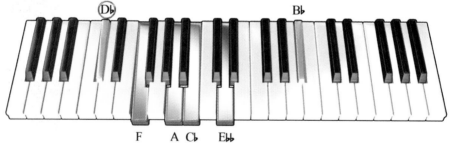

F A Cb Ebb

Db13#5#9

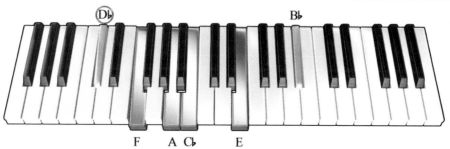

F A Cb E

Db 6/9

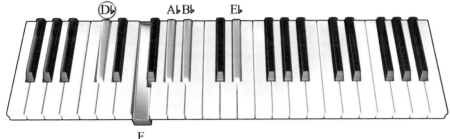

Db   Ab Bb   Eb

F

Db major9

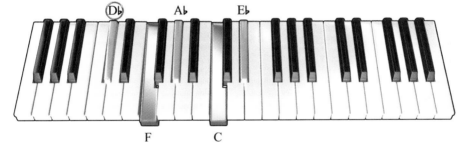

Db   Ab   Eb

F   C

Db major9#11

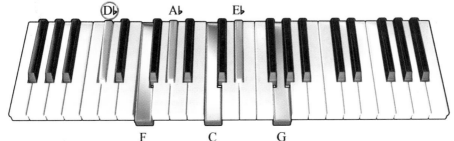

Db   Ab   Eb

F   C   G

D♭ major13

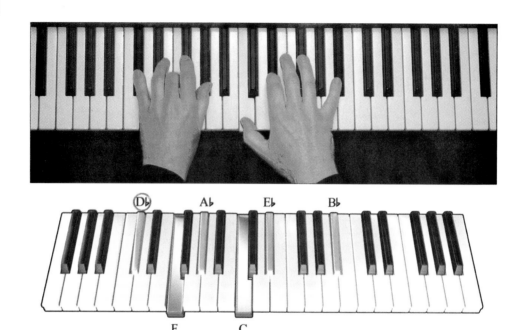

D♭ major13♭5

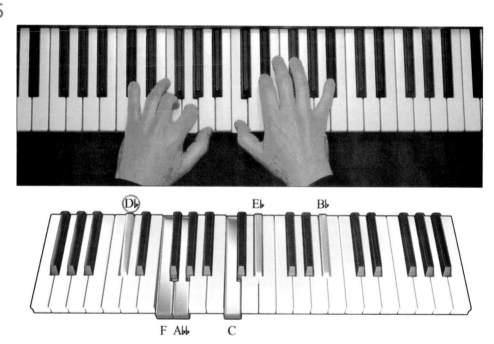

D♭ major13#5

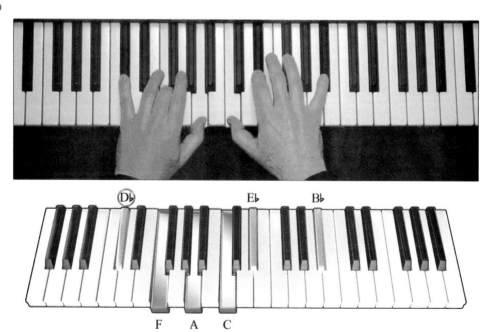

Db

Db major13b9

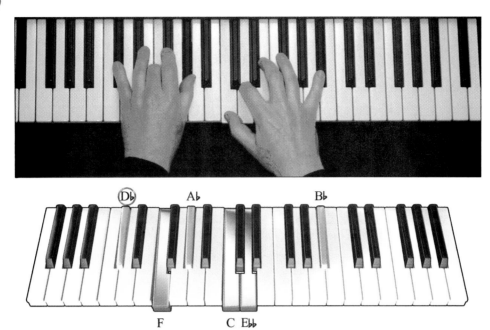

Db   Ab   Bb

F   C Ebb

Db major13#9

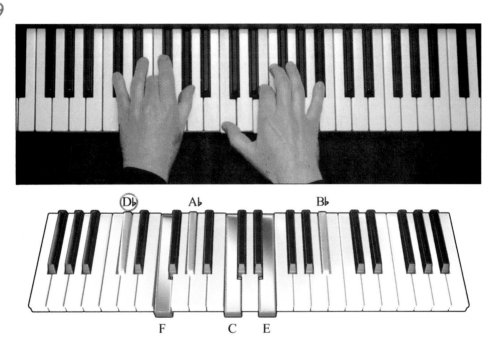

Db   Ab   Bb

F   C   E

Db major13b5b9

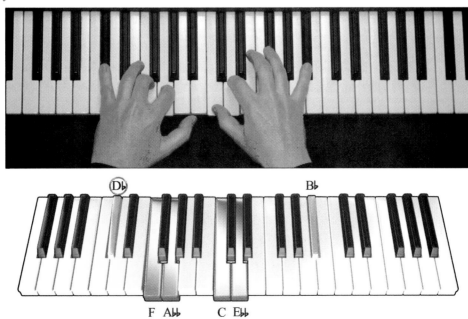

Db   Bb

F Abb   C Ebb

D♭ major13♭5#9

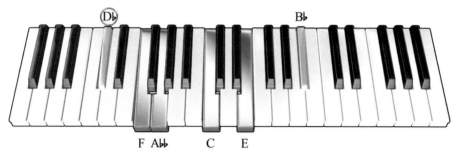

D♭ major13#5♭9

D♭ major13#5#9

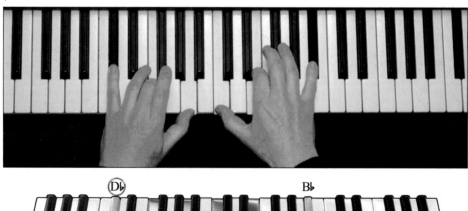

Db

Db minor7b9

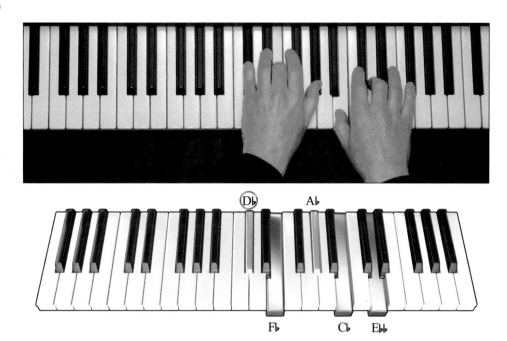

Db   Ab

Fb   Cb   Ebb

Db minor9

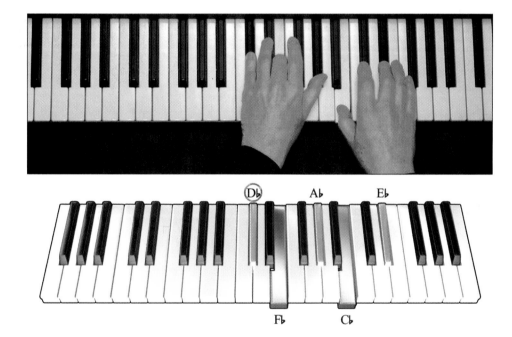

Db   Ab   Eb

Fb   Cb

Db minor11

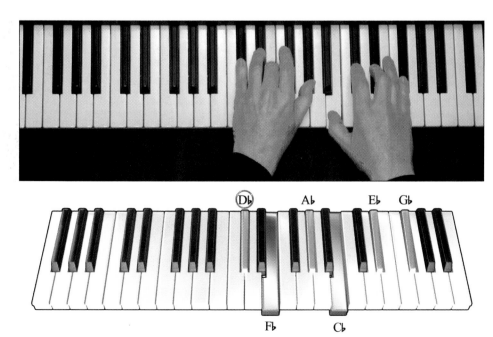

Db   Ab   Eb   Gb

Fb   Cb

D♭ minor13

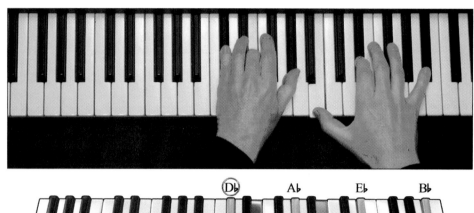

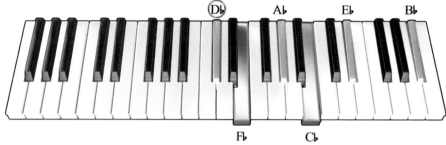

D♭ minor9 (major7)

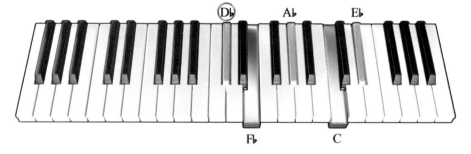

D chords

D major

D/F♯ *(first inversion)*

D/A *(second inversion)*

D augmented

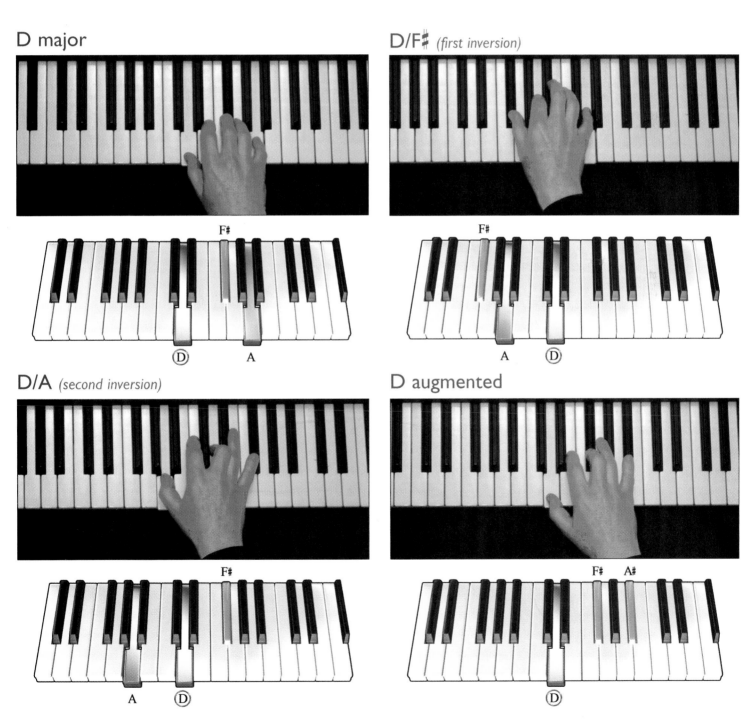

D augmented *(first inversion)*

F#   A#

Ⓓ

D augmented *(second inversion)*

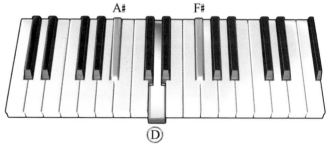

A#   F#

Ⓓ

Dsus4

Ⓓ   G   A

Dsus4 *(first inversion)*

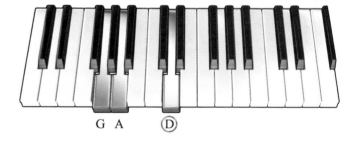

G   A   Ⓓ

Dsus4 *(second inversion)*

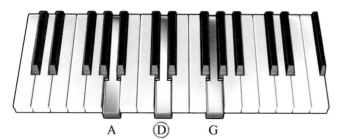

A   Ⓓ   G

D6

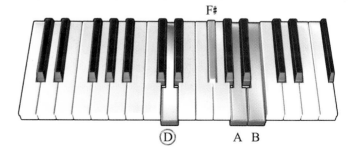

F#

Ⓓ   A B

D

D6 *(first inversion)*

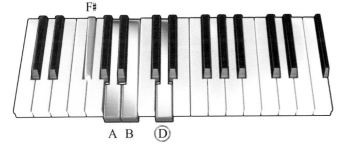

F#

A B Ⓓ

D6 *(second inversion)*

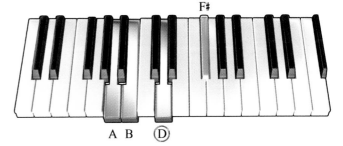

F#

A B Ⓓ

D6 *(third inversion)*

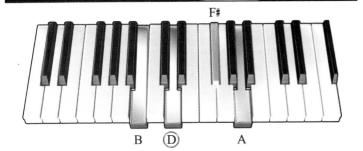

F#

B Ⓓ   A

D7

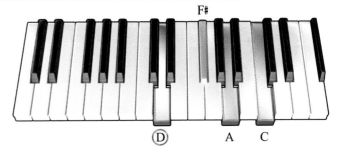

F#

Ⓓ   A   C

D7 *(first inversion)*

F#

A   C Ⓓ

D7 *(second inversion)*

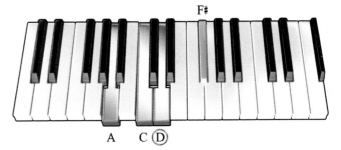

F#

A   C Ⓓ

D7 *(third inversion)*

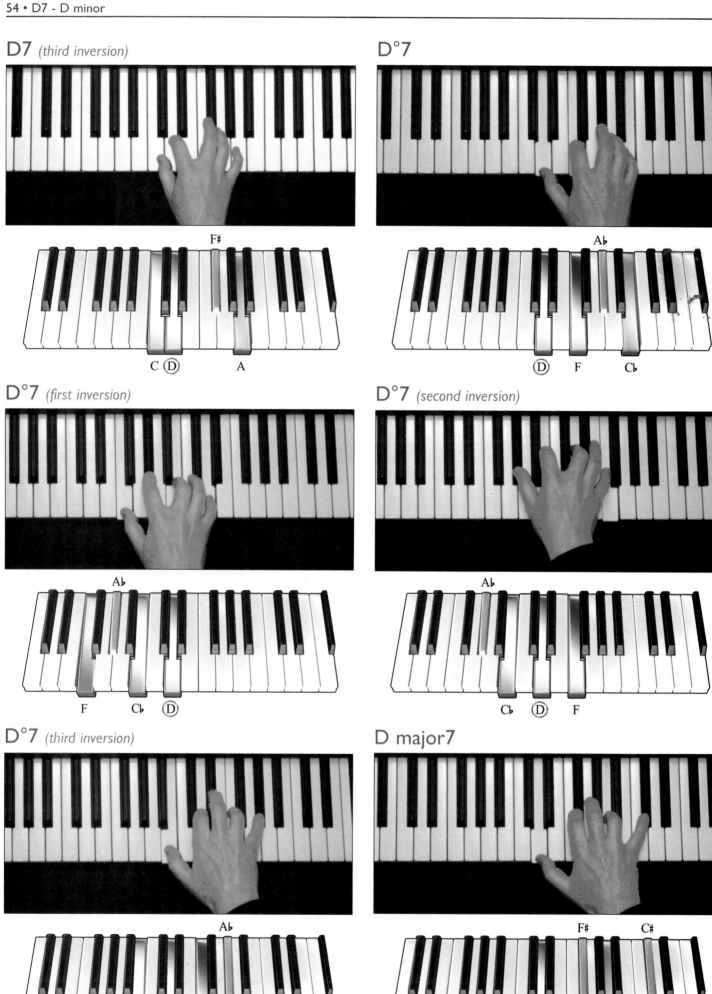

D°7

D°7 *(first inversion)*

D°7 *(second inversion)*

D°7 *(third inversion)*

D major7

D

D major7 (first inversion)

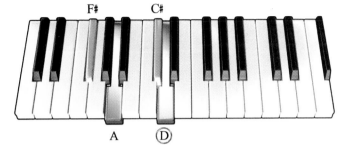

F#   C#

A   Ⓓ

D major7 (second inversion)

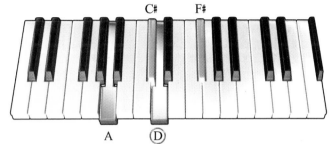

C#   F#

A   Ⓓ

D major7 (third inversion)

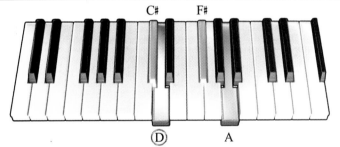

C#   F#

Ⓓ   A

D minor

Ⓓ   F   A

D minor (first inversion)

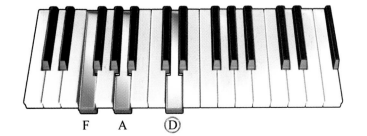

F   A   Ⓓ

D minor (second inversion)

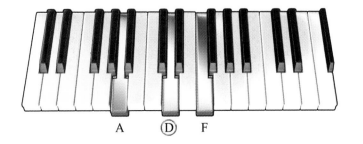

A   Ⓓ   F

D minor6

Ⓓ F A B

D minor6 *(first inversion)*

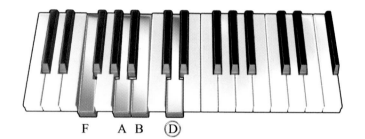

F A B Ⓓ

D minor6 *(second inversion)*

A B Ⓓ F

D minor6 *(third inversion)*

B Ⓓ F A

D minor7

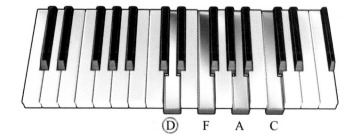

Ⓓ F A C

D minor7 *(first inversion)*

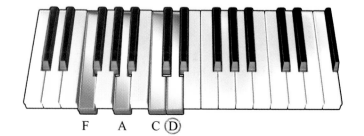

F A C Ⓓ

D minor7 *(second inversion)*

A   C Ⓓ   F

D minor7 *(third inversion)*

C Ⓓ   F   A

D minor7♭5

A♭

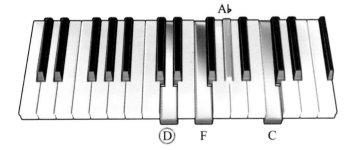

Ⓓ   F   C

D minor7♭5 *(first inversion)*

A♭

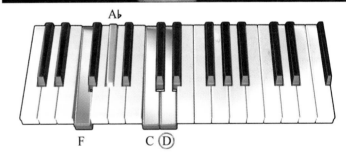

F   C Ⓓ

D minor7♭5 *(second inversion)*

A♭

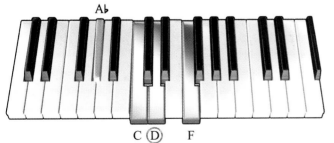

C Ⓓ   F

D minor7♭5 *(third inversion)*

A♭

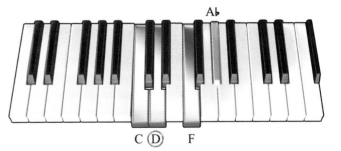

C Ⓓ   F

D minor (major7)

C#

D F A

D minor (major7) *(first inversion)*

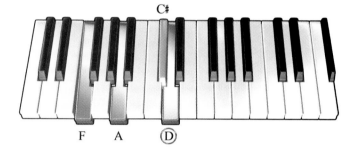

C#

F A D

D minor (major7) *(second inversion)*

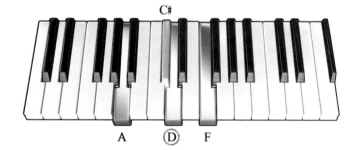

C#

A D F

D minor (major7) *(third inversion)*

C#

D F A

D chords
using both hands

D7♭9

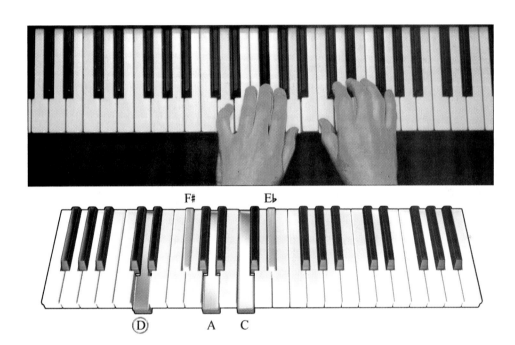

F#   E♭

Ⓓ   A   C

D7♯9

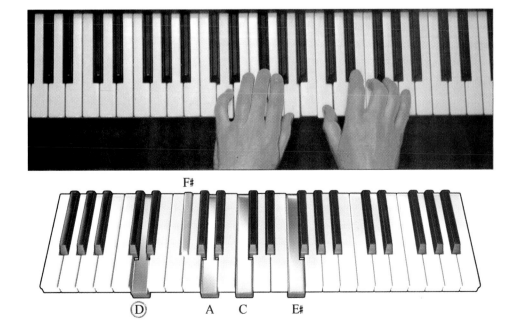

F#

Ⓓ   A   C   E♯

D9

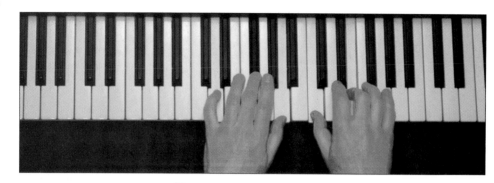

D9sus4

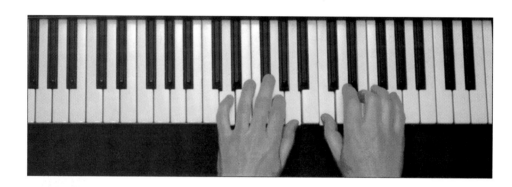

D9♭5

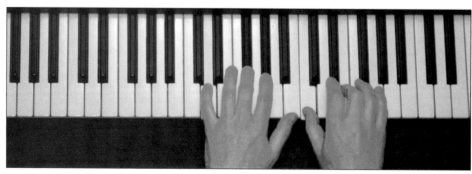

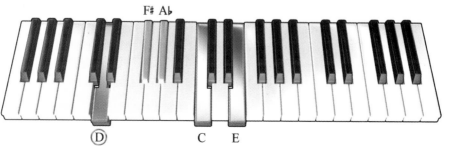

D9#5

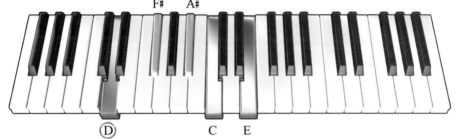

F#   A#

D   C   E

D9#11

F#   G#

D   A   C   E

D13

F#

D   A   C   E   B

D13sus4

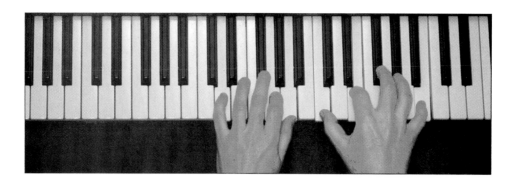

Ⓓ   G A   C   E   B

D13♭5

F# A♭

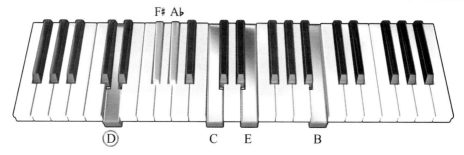

Ⓓ   C   E   B

D13♯5

F#   A#

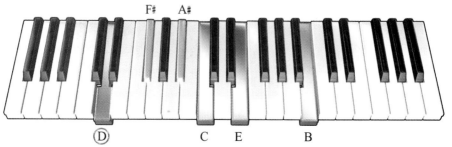

Ⓓ   C   E   B

D13♭9

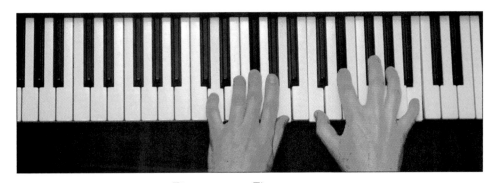

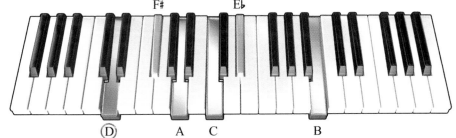

F#   E♭

Ⓓ   A   C   B

D13♯9

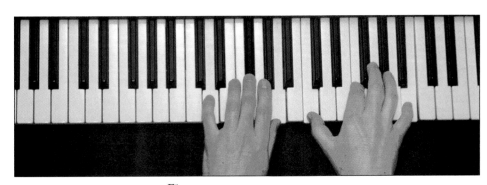

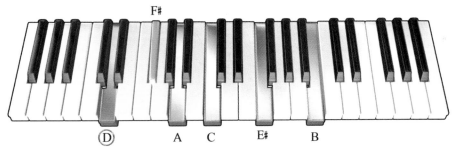

F#

Ⓓ   A   C   E#   B

D13♭5♭9

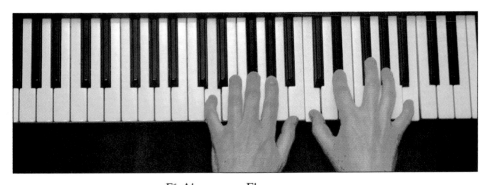

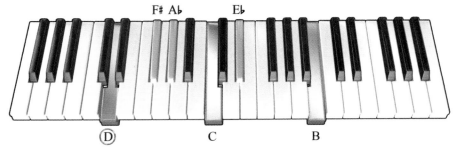

F# A♭   E♭

Ⓓ   C   B

D

D13♭5♯9

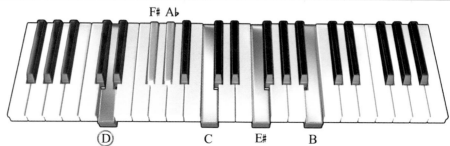

F# A♭

D   C   E#   B

D13♯5♭9

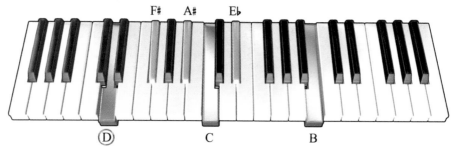

F#   A#   E♭

D   C   B

D13♯5♯9

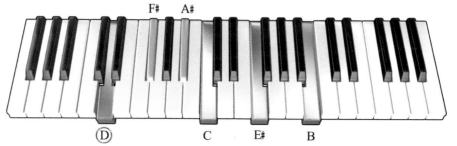

F#   A#

D   C   E#   B

D

D 6/9

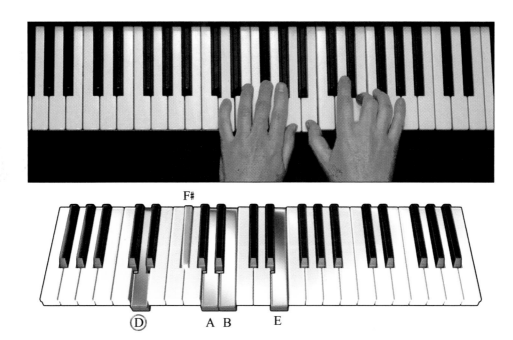

F#

D̂   A B   E

D major9

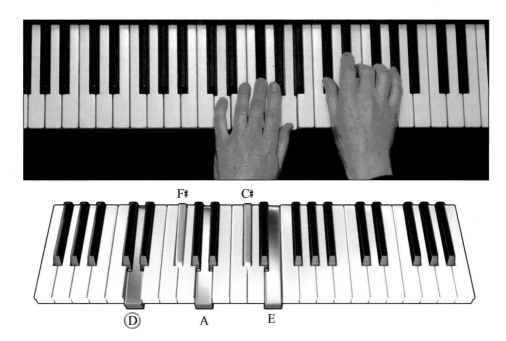

F#   C#

D̂   A   E

D major9♯11

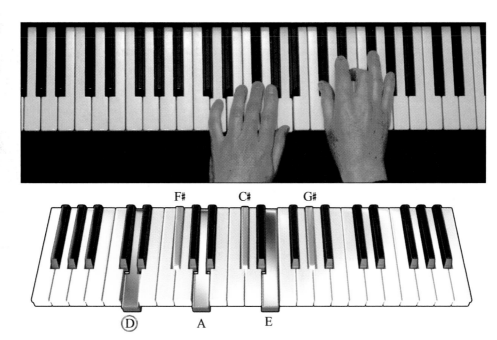

F#   C#   G#

D̂   A   E

D major13

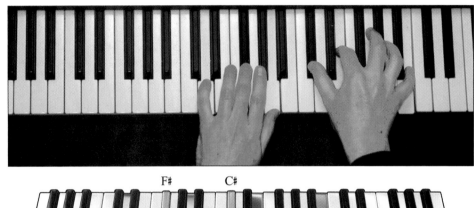

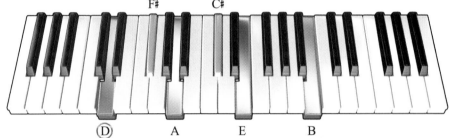

D major13♭5

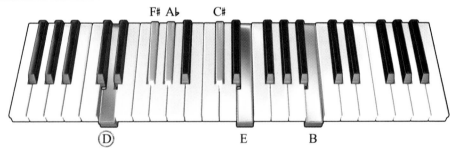

D major13♯5

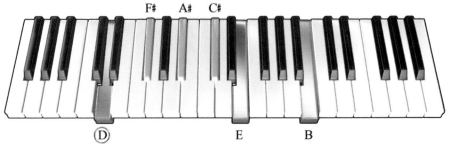

D major13♭9

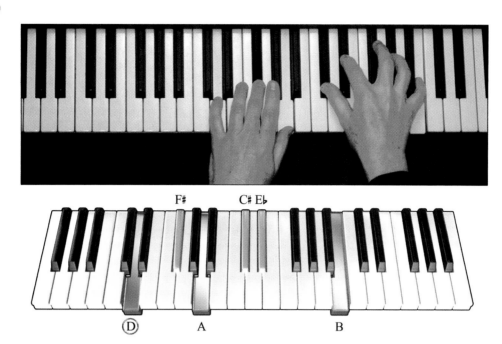

F#   C# E♭

D   A   B

D major13♯9

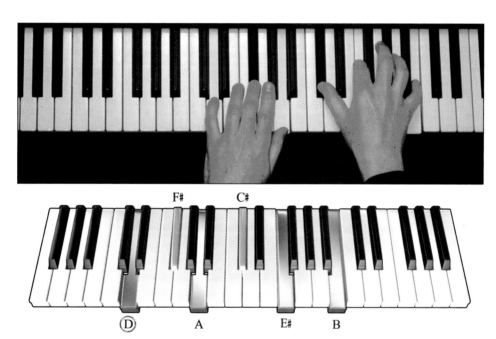

F#   C#

D   A   E#   B

D major13♭5♭9

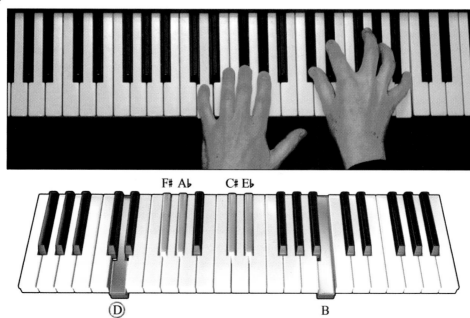

F# A♭   C# E♭

D   B

D

D major13♭5♯9

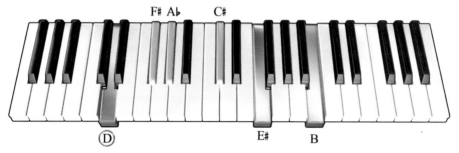

D major13♯5♭9

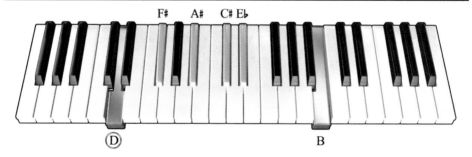

D major13♯5♯9

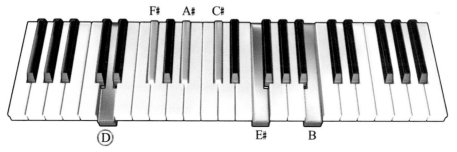

D minor7♭9

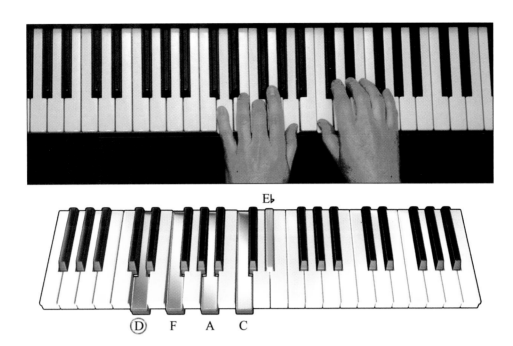

E♭

Ⓓ   F   A   C

D minor9

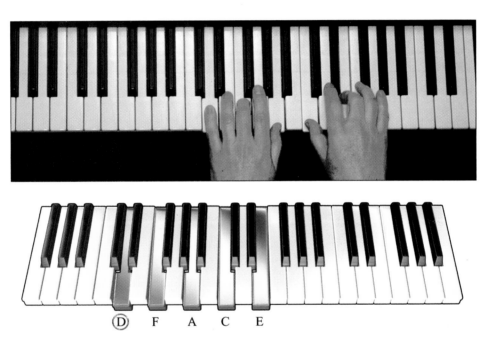

Ⓓ   F   A   C   E

D minor11

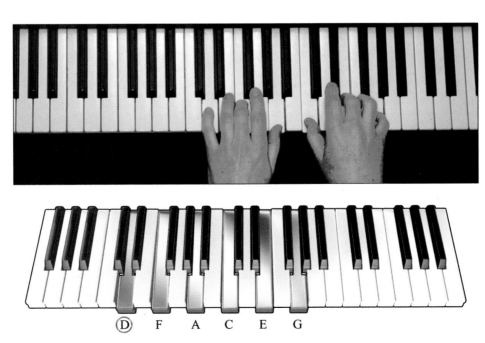

Ⓓ   F   A   C   E   G

D minor13

Ⓓ F A C E B

D minor9 (major7)

C♯

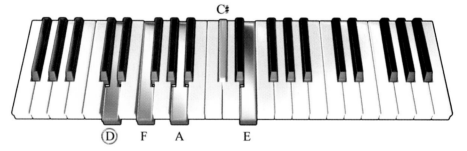

Ⓓ F A E

E♭ chords

E♭ major

E♭   B♭

E♭/G *(first inversion)*

B♭   E♭

G

E♭/B♭ *(second inversion)*

B♭   E♭

G

E♭ augmented

E♭

G   B

Eb augmented *(first inversion)*

G   B   Eb

Eb augmented *(second inversion)*

Eb   B   G

Ebsus4

Eb   Ab Bb

Ebsus4 *(first inversion)*

Ab Bb   Eb

Ebsus4 *(second inversion)*

Bb   Eb   Ab

Eb6

Eb   Bb
G   C

E♭6 *(first inversion)*

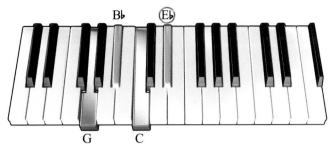

B♭   (E♭)

G   C

E♭6 *(second inversion)*

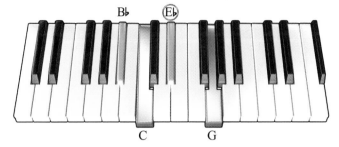

B♭   (E♭)

C   G

E♭6 *(third inversion)*

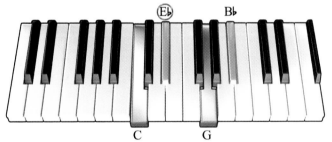

(E♭)   B♭

C   G

E♭7

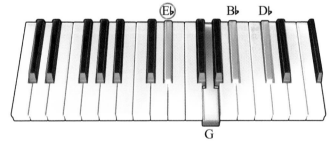

(E♭)   B♭   D♭

G

E♭7 *(first inversion)*

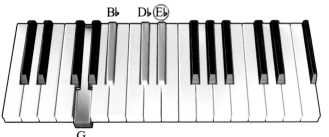

B♭   D♭(E♭)

G

E♭7 *(second inversion)*

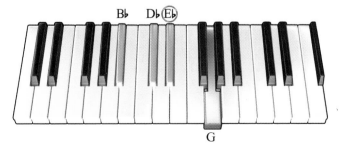

B♭   D♭(E♭)

G

E♭

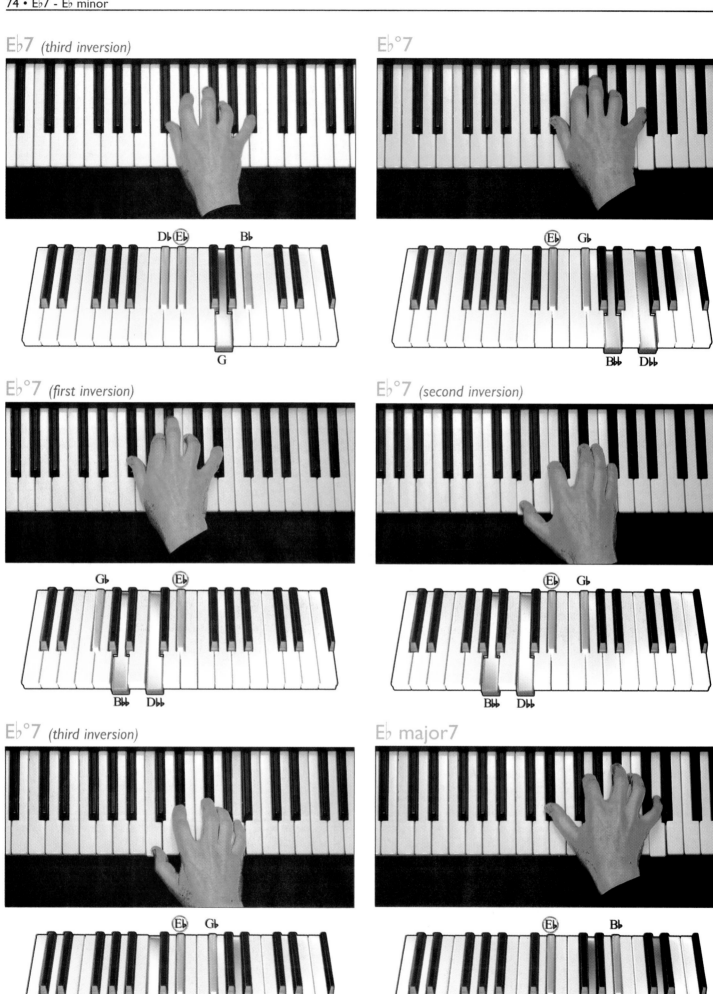

E♭7 *(third inversion)*

E♭°7

E♭°7 *(first inversion)*

E♭°7 *(second inversion)*

E♭°7 *(third inversion)*

E♭ major7

E♭ major7 (first inversion)

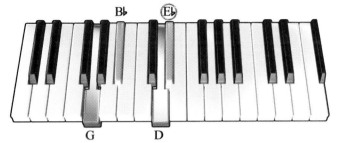

B♭   (E♭)

G   D

E♭ major7 (second inversion)

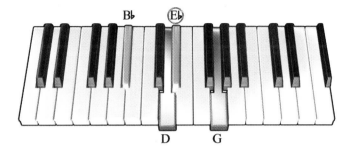

B♭   (E♭)

D   G

E♭ major7 (third inversion)

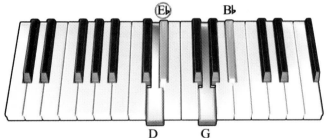

(E♭)   B♭

D   G

E♭ minor

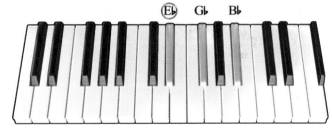

(E♭)   G♭   B♭

E♭ minor (first inversion)

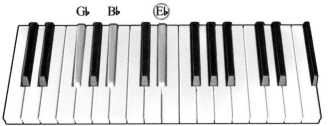

G♭   B♭   (E♭)

E♭ minor (second inversion)

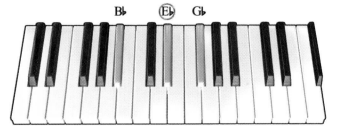

B♭   (E♭)   G♭

E♭

E♭ minor6

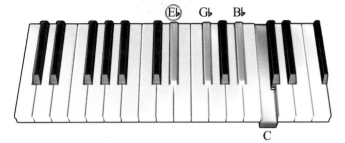

E♭ minor6 *(first inversion)*

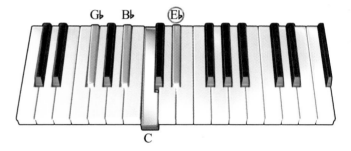

E♭ minor6 *(second inversion)*

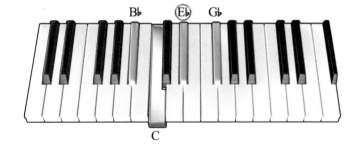

E♭ minor6 *(third inversion)*

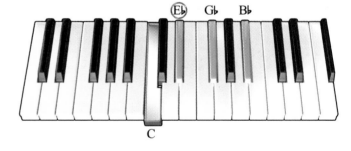

E♭ minor7

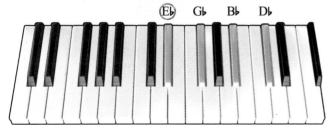

E♭ minor7 *(first inversion)*

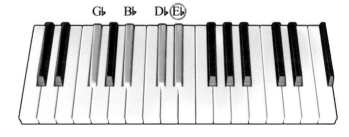

E♭ minor7 *(second inversion)*

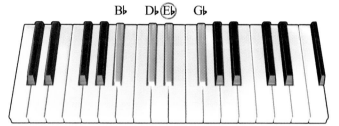

B♭ D♭ (E♭) G♭

E♭ minor7 *(third inversion)*

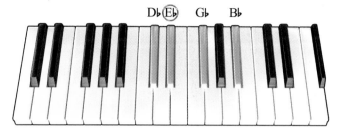

D♭ (E♭) G♭ B♭

E♭

E♭ minor7♭5

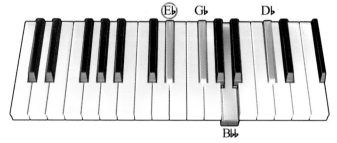

(E♭) G♭ D♭

B♭♭

E♭ minor7♭5 *(first inversion)*

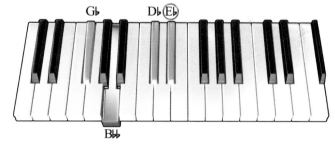

G♭ D♭(E♭)

B♭♭

E♭ minor7♭5 *(second inversion)*

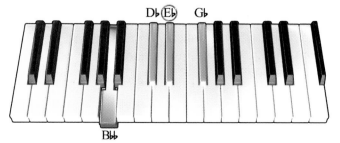

D♭(E♭) G♭

B♭♭

E♭ minor7♭5 *(third inversion)*

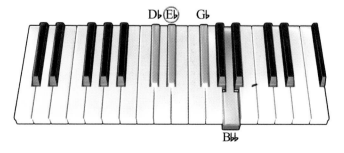

D♭(E♭) G♭

B♭♭

E♭ minor (major7)

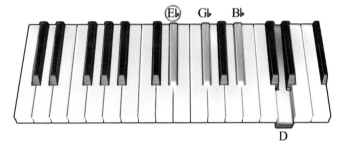

E♭ minor (major7) *(first inversion)*

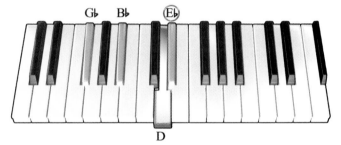

E♭ minor (major7) *(second inversion)*

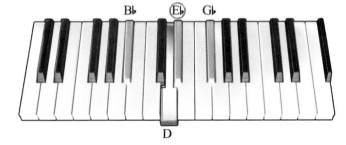

E♭ minor (major7) *(third inversion)*

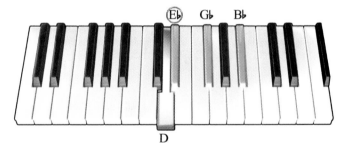

E♭ chords
using both hands

E♭7♭9

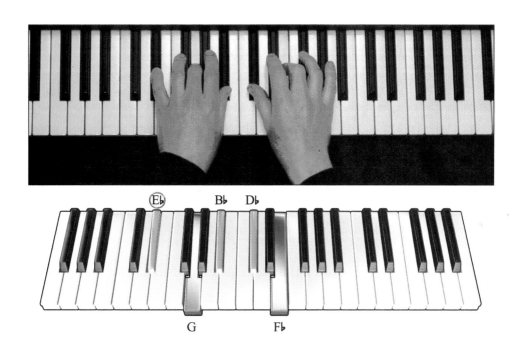

E♭7♯9

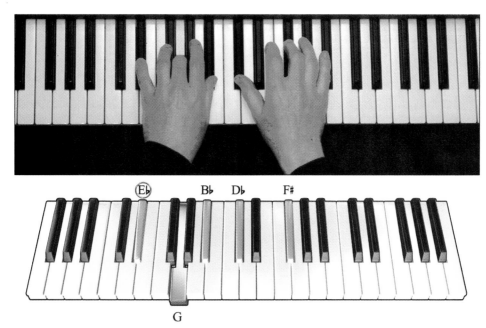

E♭9

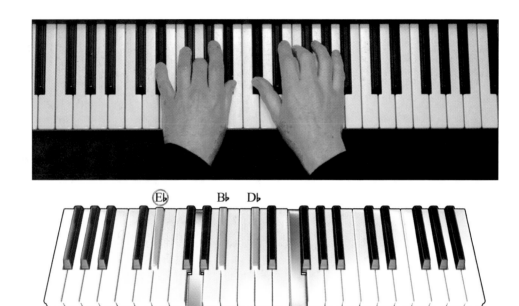

E♭9sus4

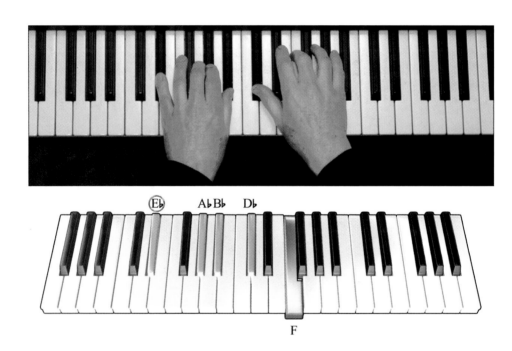

E♭9♭5

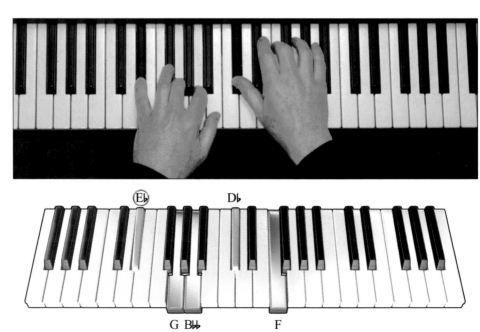

Eb9#5

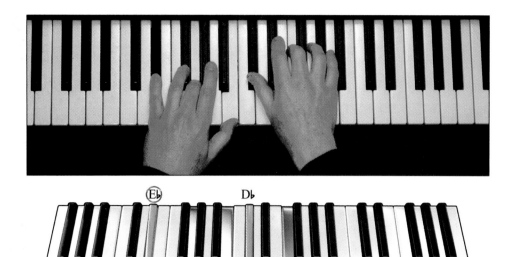

Eb   Db

G   B   F

Eb

Eb9#11

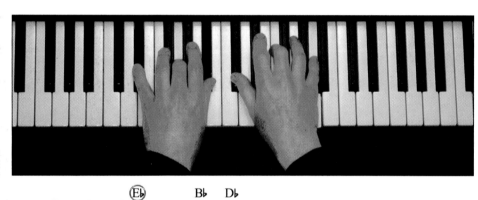

Eb   Bb   Db

G   F   A

Eb13

Eb   Bb   Db

G   F   C

Eb13sus4

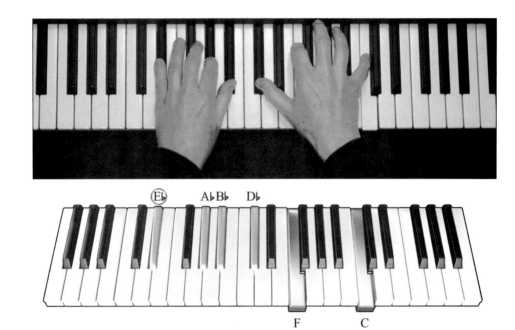

Eb   Ab Bb   Db

F   C

Eb13b5

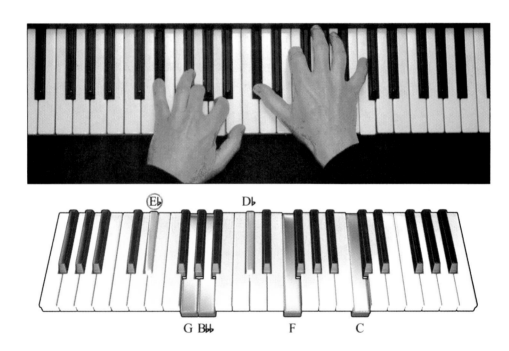

Eb   Db

G Bbb   F   C

Eb13#5

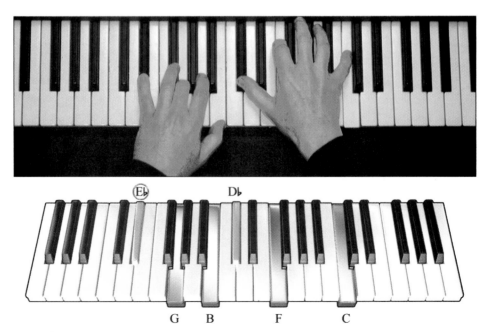

Eb   Db

G   B   F   C

Eb13b9

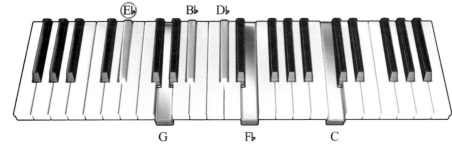

Eb13#9

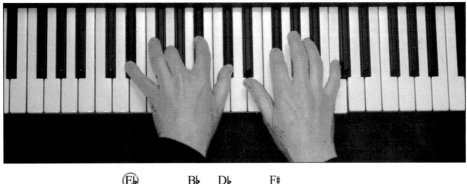

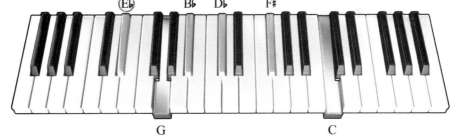

Eb13b5b9

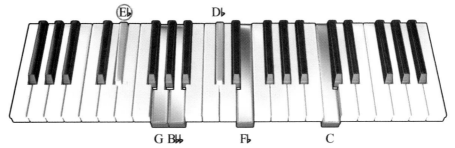

Eb

Eb13b5#9

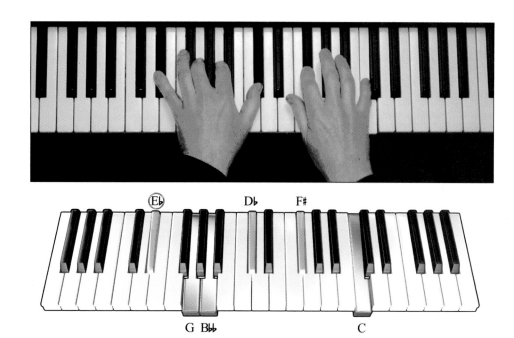

Eb13#5b9

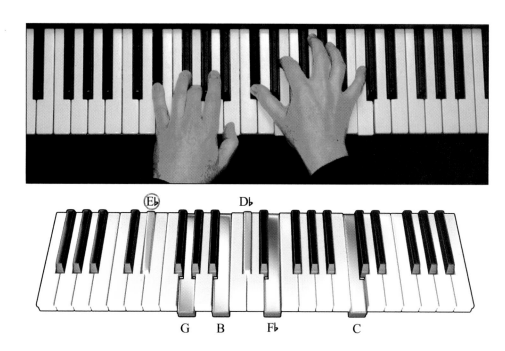

Eb13#5#9

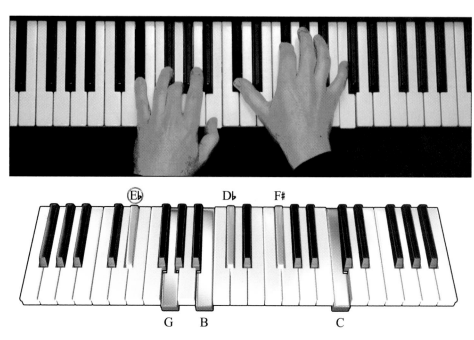

Eb 6/9

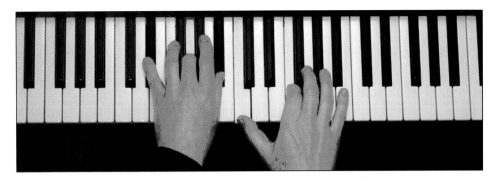

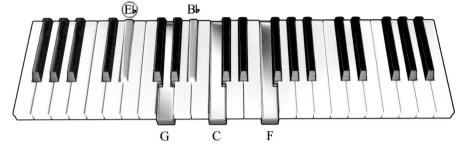

Eb major9

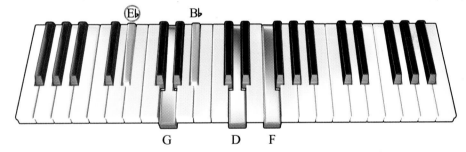

Eb major9#11

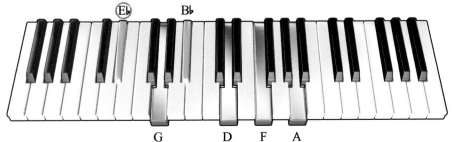

Eb

E♭ major13

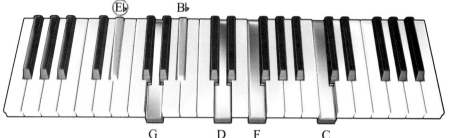

E♭ major13♭5

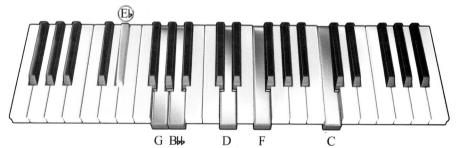

E♭ major13#5

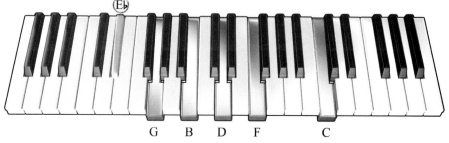

E♭ major13♭9

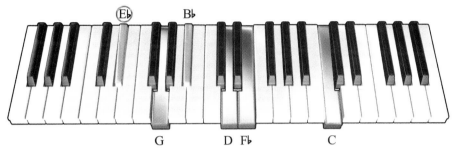

E♭ major13♯9

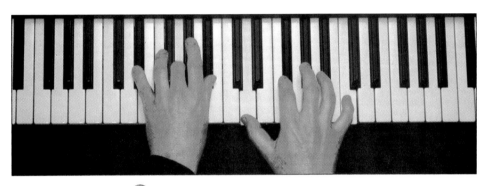

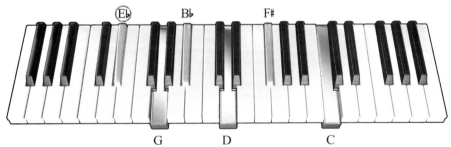

E♭ major13♭5♭9

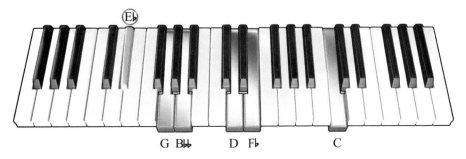

E♭

Eb major13b5#9

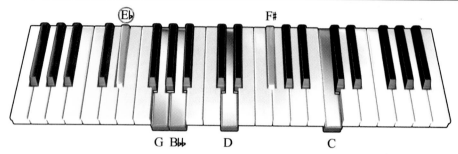

Eb   F#

G Bbb   D   C

Eb major13#5b9

Eb

G   B   D Fb   C

Eb major13#5#9

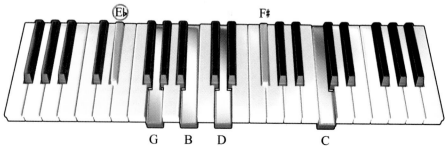

Eb   F#

G   B   D   C

E♭ minor7♭9

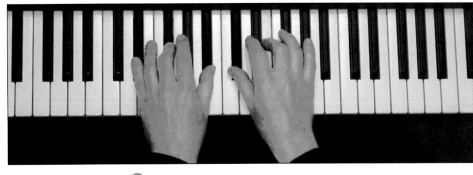

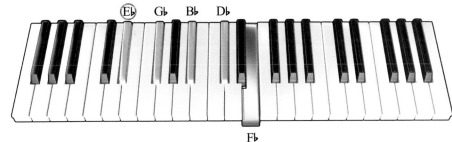

E♭ G♭ B♭ D♭

F♭

E♭ minor9

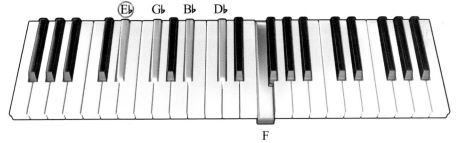

E♭ G♭ B♭ D♭

F

E♭ minor11

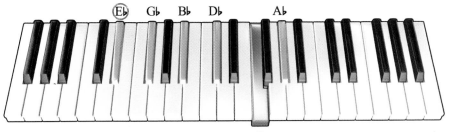

E♭ G♭ B♭ D♭ A♭

F

E♭

E♭ minor13

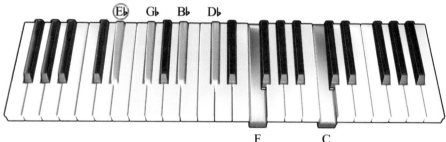

E♭ minor9 (major7)

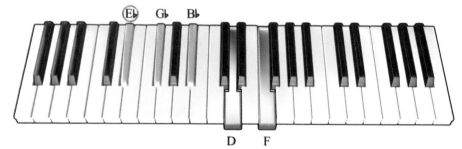

E♭ minor13

E chords

E major

E/G♯ *(first inversion)*

E/B *(second inversion)*

E augmented

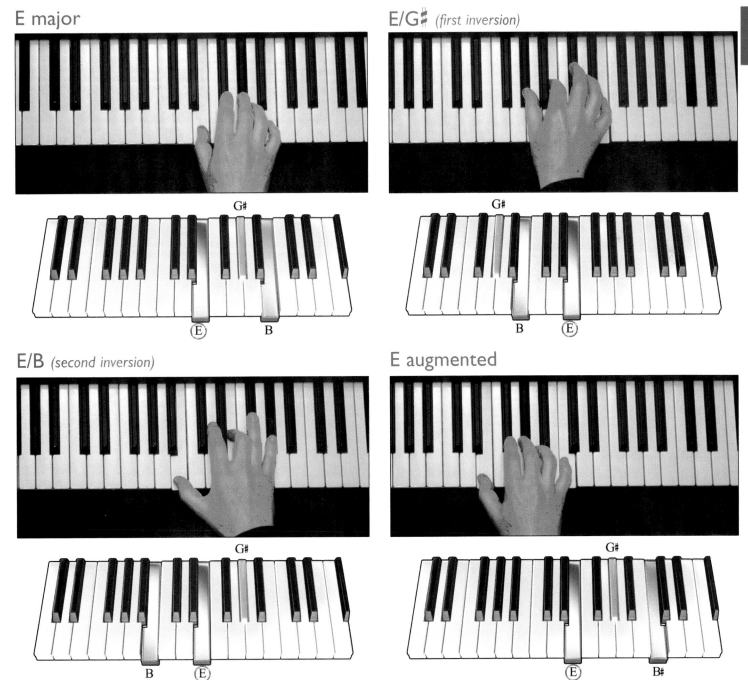

E augmented *(first inversion)*

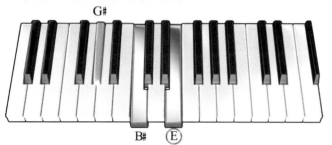

G#

B#   (E)

E augmented *(second inversion)*

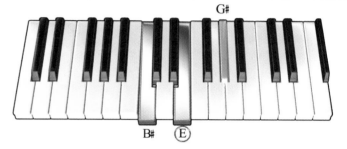

G#

B#   (E)

Esus4

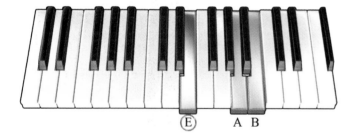

(E)   A   B

Esus4 *(first inversion)*

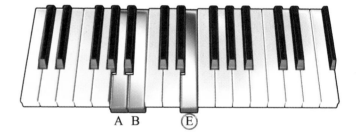

A   B   (E)

Esus4 *(second inversion)*

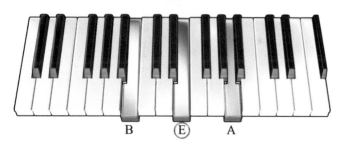

B   (E)   A

E6

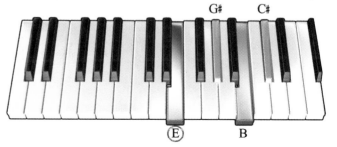

G#   C#

(E)   B

E6 *(first inversion)*

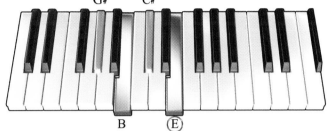

G#   C#

B   (E)

E6 *(second inversion)*

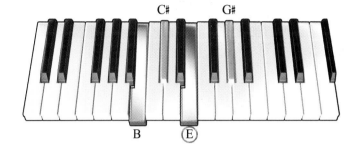

C#   G#

B   (E)

E6 *(third inversion)*

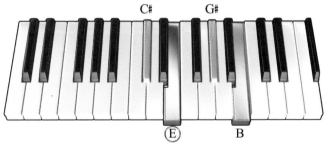

C#   G#

(E)   B

E7

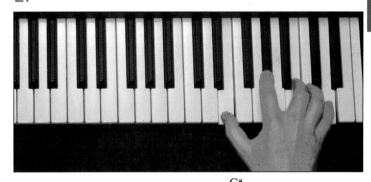

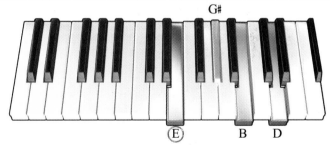

G#

(E)   B   D

E7 *(first inversion)*

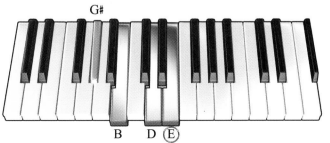

G#

B   D   (E)

E7 *(second inversion)*

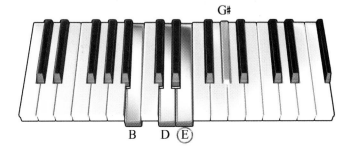

G#

B   D   (E)

E

E7 *(third inversion)*

E°7

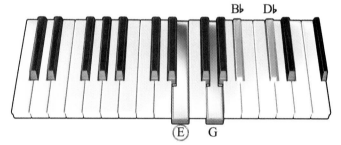

E°7 *(first inversion)*

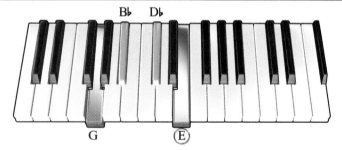

E°7 *(second inversion)*

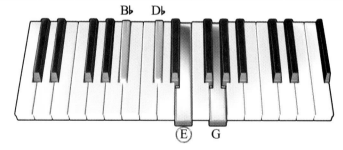

E°7 *(third inversion)*

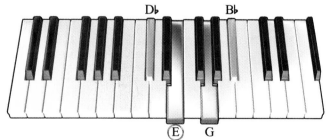

E major7

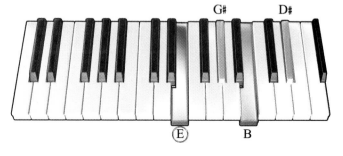

E major7 *(first inversion)*

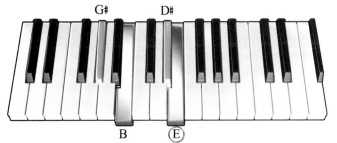

G#   D#

B   E

E major7 *(second inversion)*

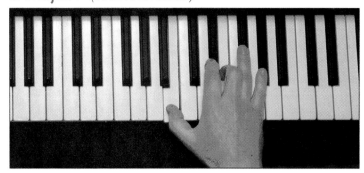

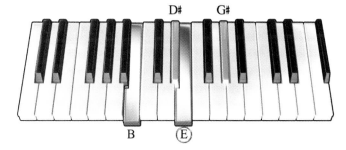

D#   G#

B   E

E major7 *(third inversion)*

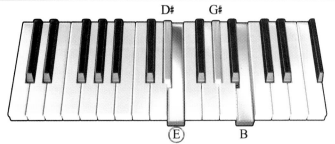

D#   G#

E   B

E minor

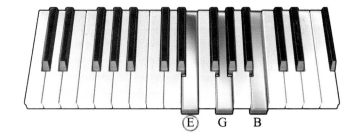

E   G   B

E minor *(first inversion)*

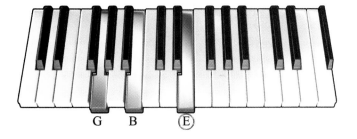

G   B   E

E minor *(second inversion)*

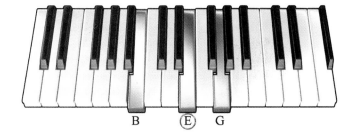

B   E   G

E

E minor6

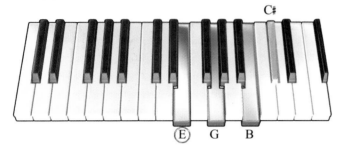

E G B

C#

E minor6 *(first inversion)*

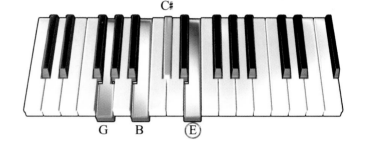

G B E

C#

E minor6 *(second inversion)*

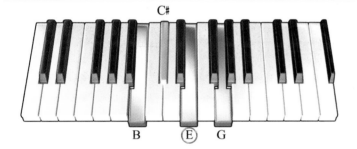

B E G

C#

E minor6 *(third inversion)*

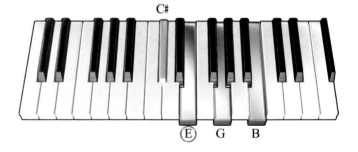

E G B

C#

E minor7

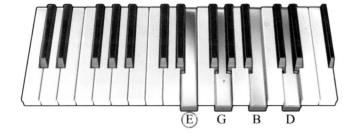

E G B D

E minor7 *(first inversion)*

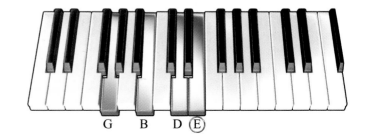

G B D E

E minor7 *(second inversion)*

B D (E) G

E minor7 *(third inversion)*

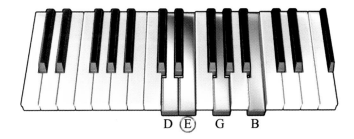

D (E) G B

E

E minor7♭5

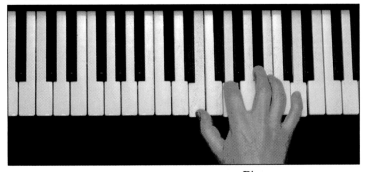
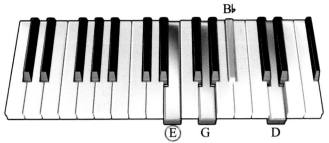

B♭

(E) G D

E minor7♭5 *(first inversion)*

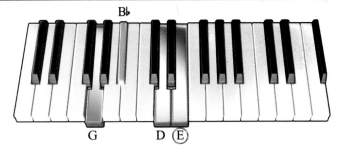

B♭

G D (E)

E minor7♭5 *(second inversion)*

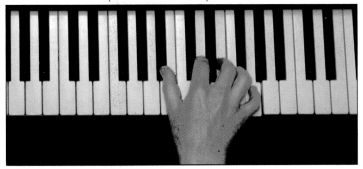

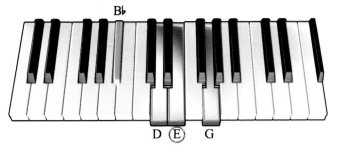

B♭

D (E) G

E minor7♭5 *(third inversion)*

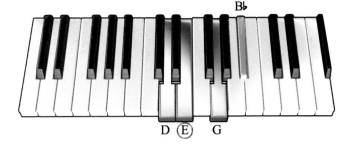

B♭

D (E) G

E minor (major7)

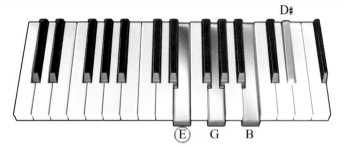

E minor (major7) *(first inversion)*

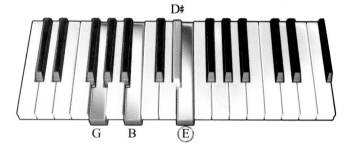

E minor (major7) *(second inversion)*

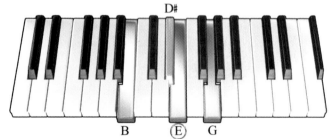

E minor (major7) *(third inversion)*

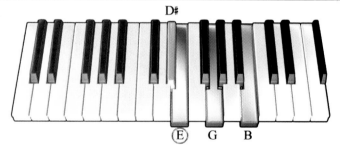

E chords
using both hands

E7♭9

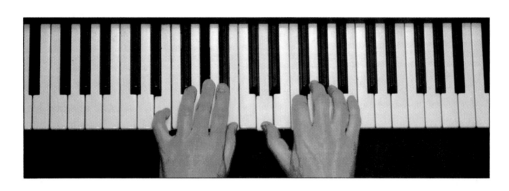

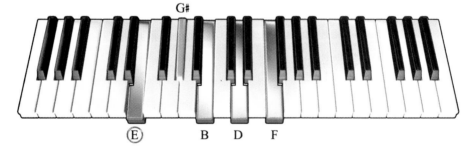

G#

Ⓔ   B   D   F

E7♯9

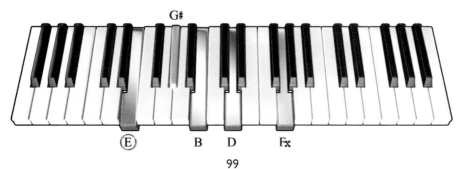

G#

Ⓔ   B   D   F𝘹

E

E9

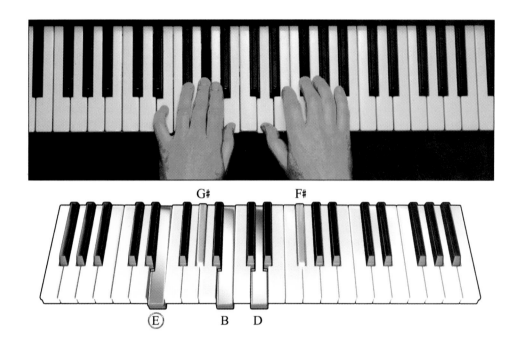

E9sus4

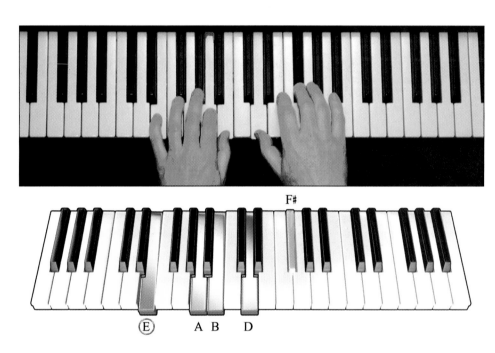

E9♭5

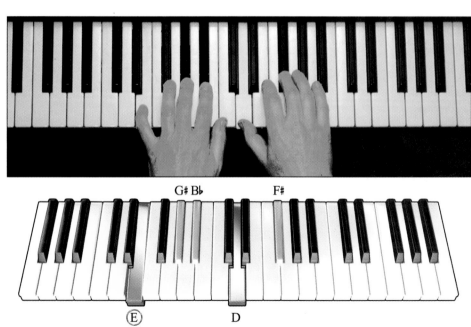

E9#5

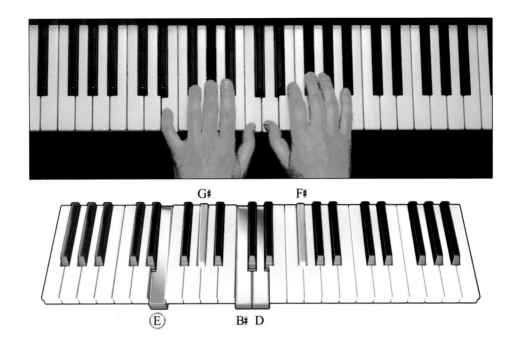

G#   F#

Ⓔ   B# D

E9#11

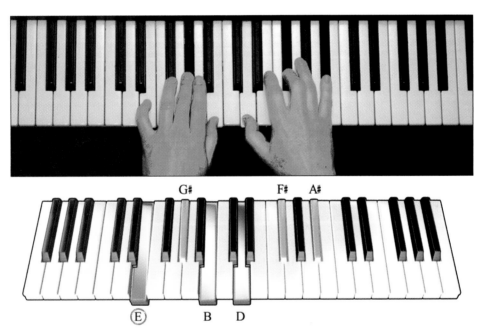

G#   F#   A#

Ⓔ   B   D

E13

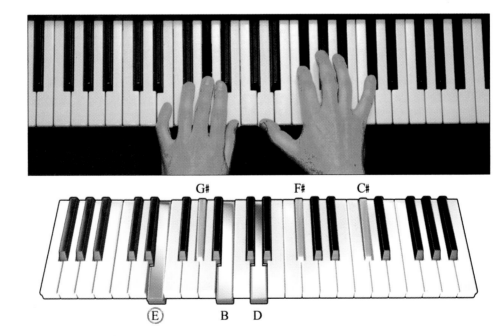

G#   F#   C#

Ⓔ   B   D

E

E13sus4

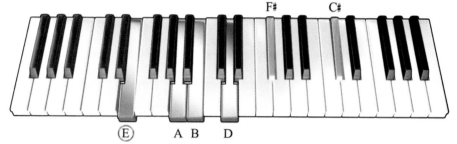

F#   C#

Ⓔ   A B   D

E13♭5

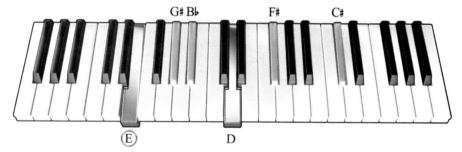

G# B♭   F#   C#

Ⓔ   D

E13#5

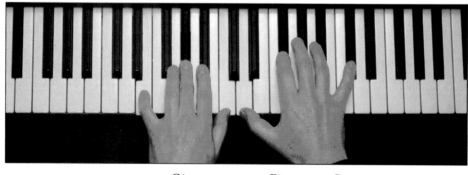

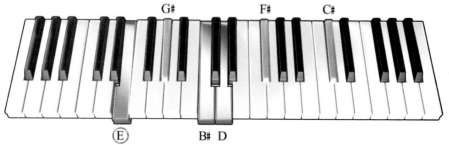

G#   F#   C#

Ⓔ   B# D

E13♭9

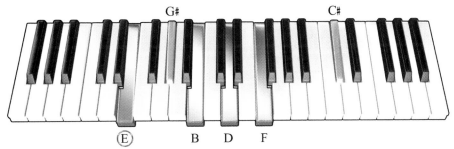

G#   C#

Ⓔ   B   D   F

E13♯9

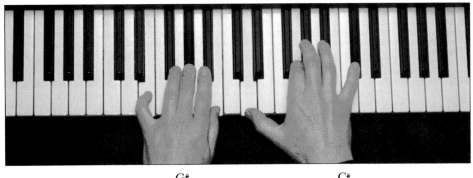

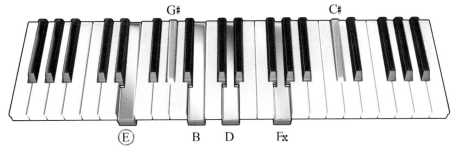

G#   C#

Ⓔ   B   D   F𝗑

E13♭5♭9

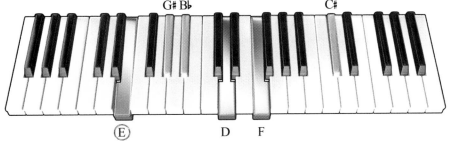

G# B♭   C#

Ⓔ   D   F

E

E13♭5♯9

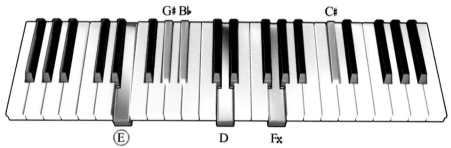

E13♯5♭9

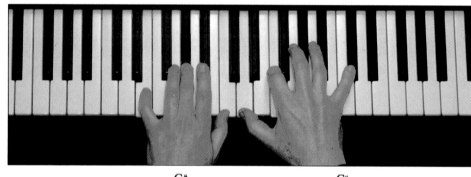

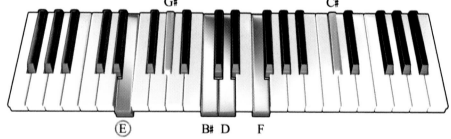

E13♯5♯9

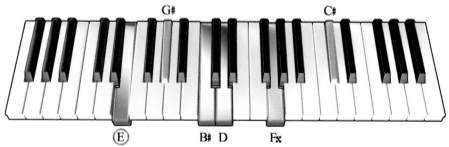

E 6/9

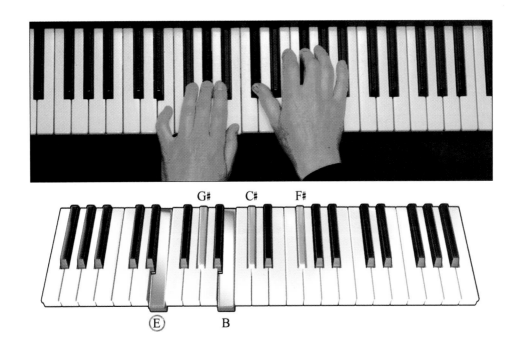

G#   C#   F#

Ⓔ   B

E major9

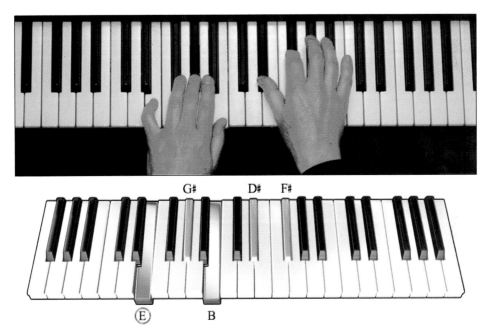

G#   D# F#

Ⓔ   B

E major9#11

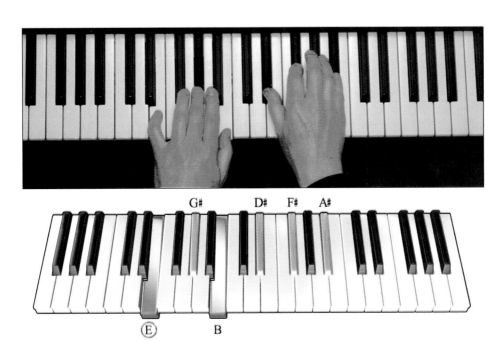

G#   D# F# A#

Ⓔ   B

E

E major13

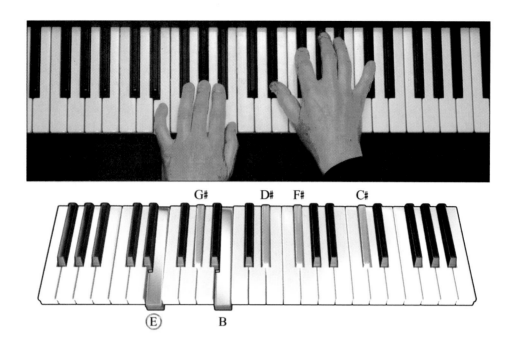

G#   D#   F#   C#

Ⓔ   B

E major13♭5

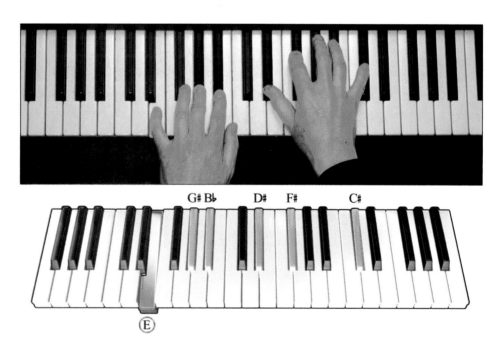

G# B♭   D#   F#   C#

Ⓔ

E major13♯5

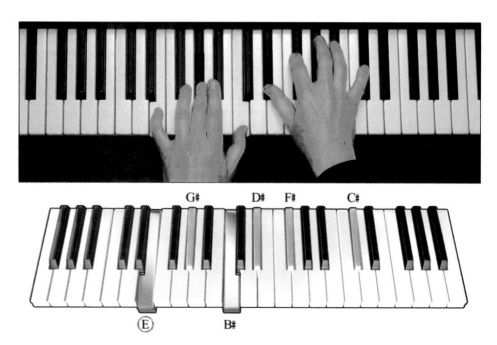

G#   D#   F#   C#

Ⓔ   B#

E major13♭9

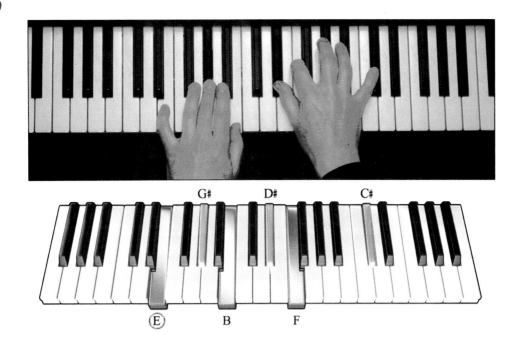

G#   D#   C#

(E)   B   F

E major13♯9

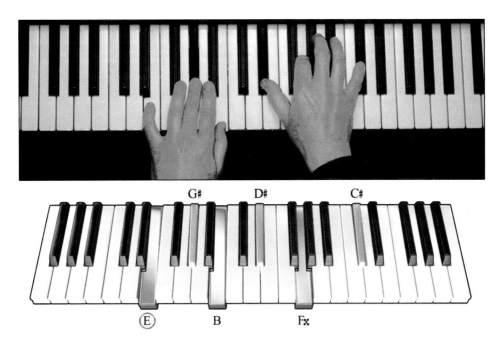

G#   D#   C#

(E)   B   F𝄪

E major13♭5♭9

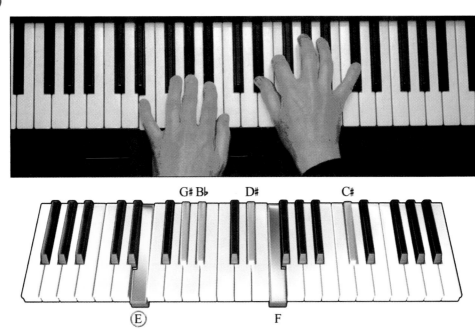

G# B♭   D#   C#

(E)   F

E

E major13♭5♯9

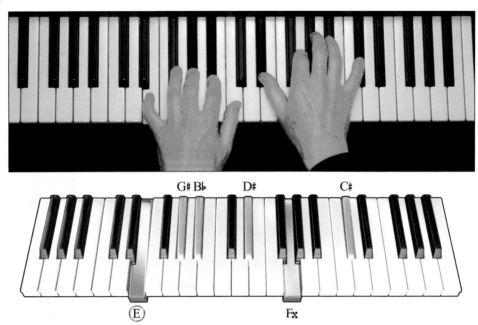

G♯ B♭   D♯   C♯

Ⓔ   F𝄪

E major13♯5♭9

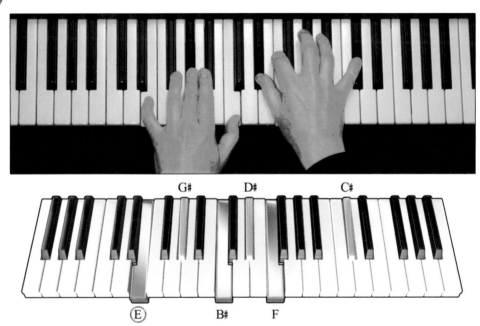

G♯   D♯   C♯

Ⓔ   B♯   F

E major13♯5♯9

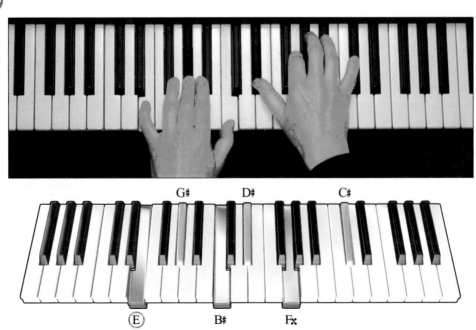

G♯   D♯   C♯

Ⓔ   B♯   F𝄪

E minor7♭9

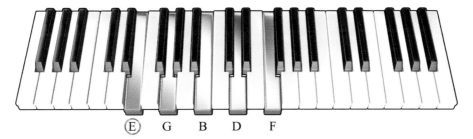

(E)   G   B   D   F

E minor9

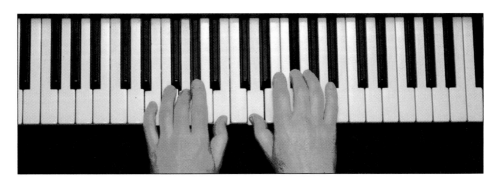

F#

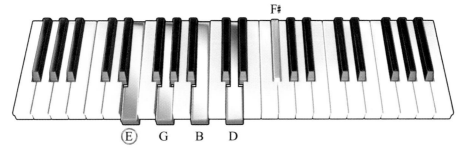

(E)   G   B   D

E minor11

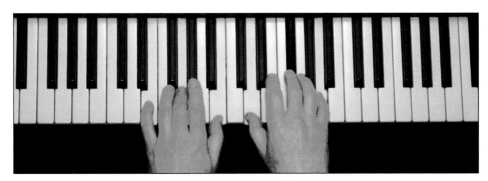

F#

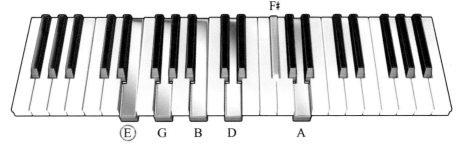

(E)   G   B   D   A

E

E minor13

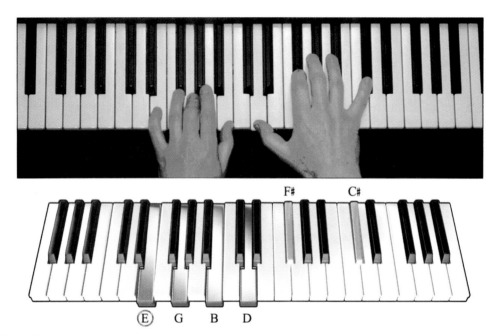

E   G   B   D   F#   C#

E minor9 (major7)

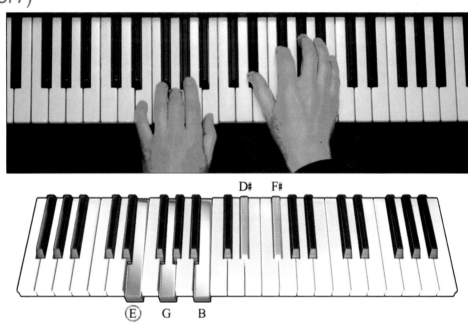

E   G   B   D#   F#

F chords

F major

F/A *(first inversion)*

F/C *(second inversion)*

F augmented

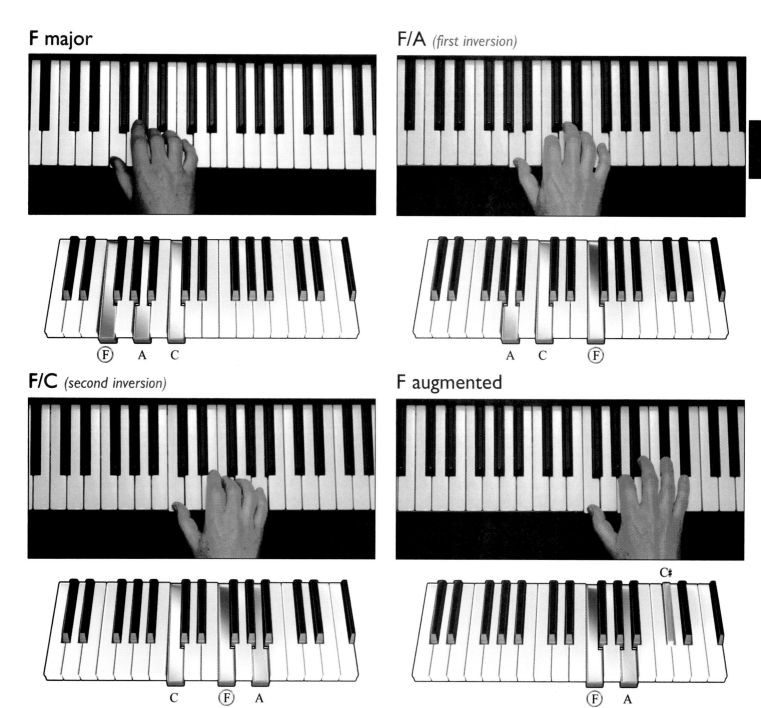

F

111

F augmented *(first inversion)*

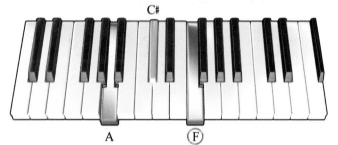

C#

A   Ⓕ

F augmented *(second inversion)*

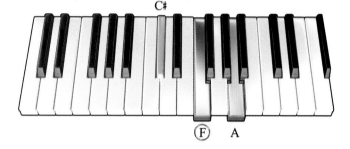

C#

Ⓕ   A

Fsus4

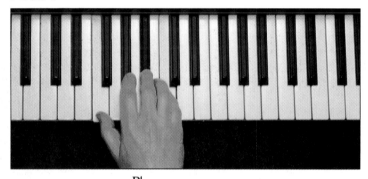

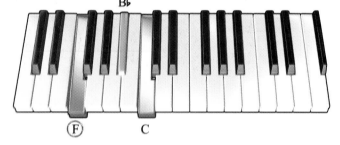

B♭

Ⓕ   C

Fsus4 *(first inversion)*

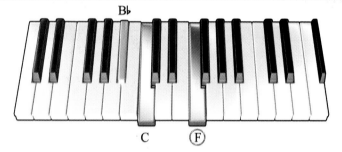

B♭

C   Ⓕ

Fsus4 *(second inversion)*

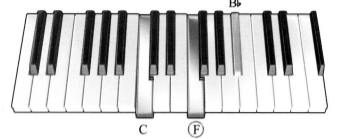

B♭

C   Ⓕ

F6

Ⓕ   A   C D

F6 *(first inversion)*

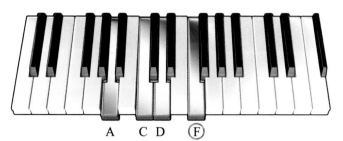

A   C   D   Ⓕ

F6 *(second inversion)*

C   D   Ⓕ   A

F6 *(third inversion)*

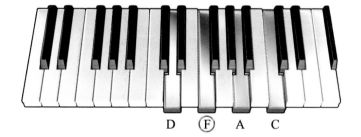

D   Ⓕ   A   C

F7

E♭

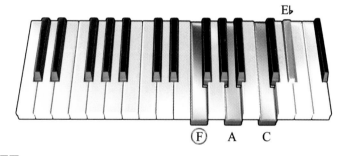

Ⓕ   A   C

F7 *(first inversion)*

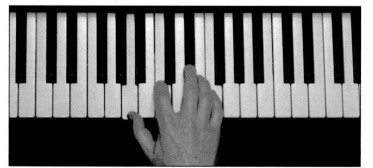

E♭

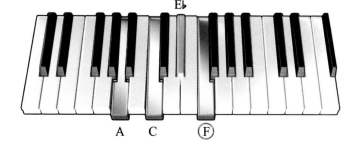

A   C   Ⓕ

F7 *(second inversion)*

E♭

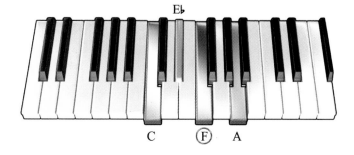

C   Ⓕ   A

F

F7 (third inversion)

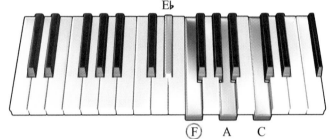

Eb

Ⓕ   A   C

F°7

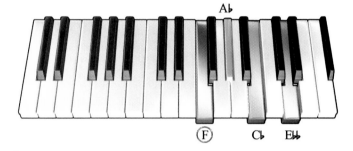

Ab

Ⓕ   Cb   Ebb

F°7 (first inversion)

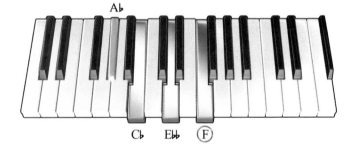

Ab

Cb   Ebb   Ⓕ

F°7 (second inversion)

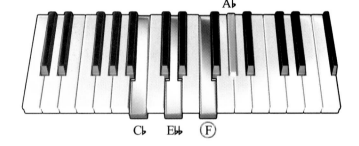

Ab

Cb   Ebb   Ⓕ

F°7 (third inversion)

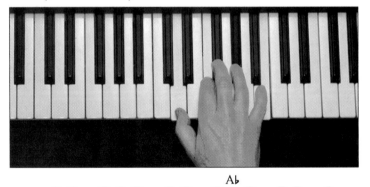

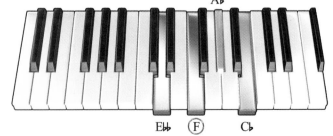

Ab

Ebb   Ⓕ   Cb

F major7

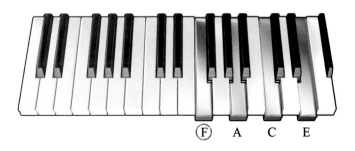

Ⓕ   A   C   E

F major7 *(first inversion)*

A　C　E　Ⓕ

F major7 *(second inversion)*

C　E　Ⓕ　A

F major7 *(third inversion)*

E　Ⓕ　A　C

F minor

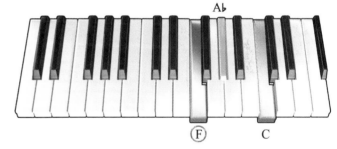

A♭

Ⓕ　　C

F minor *(first inversion)*

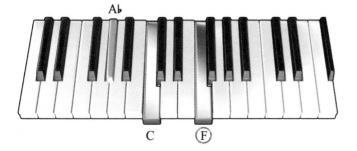

A♭

C　Ⓕ

F minor *(second inversion)*

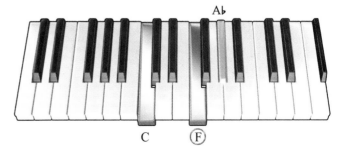

A♭

C　Ⓕ

F

F minor6

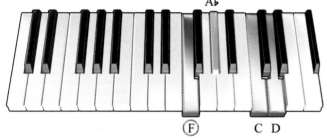

A♭

F   C D

F minor6 *(first inversion)*

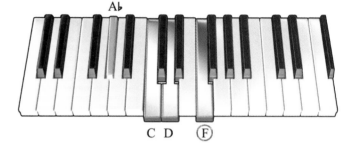

A♭

C D   F

F minor6 *(second inversion)*

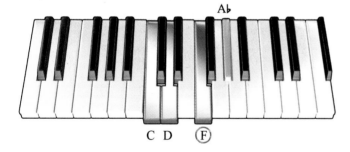

A♭

C D   F

F minor6 *(third inversion)*

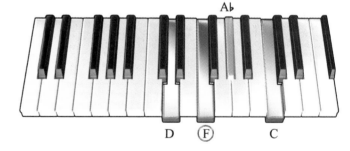

A♭

D   F   C

F minor7

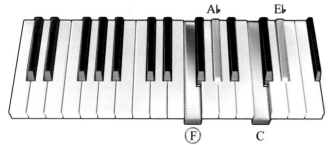

A♭   E♭

F   C

F minor7 *(first inversion)*

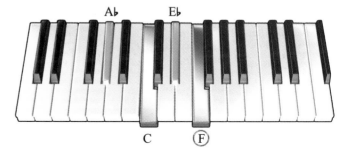

A♭   E♭

C   F

F minor7 (second inversion)

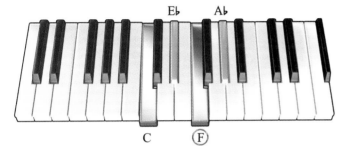

Eb   Ab

C   (F)

F minor7 (third inversion)

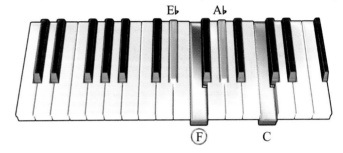

Eb   Ab

(F)   C

F minor7b5

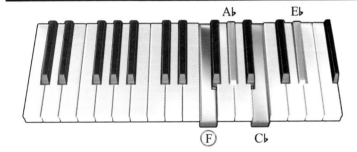

Ab   Eb

(F)   Cb

F minor7b5 (first inversion)

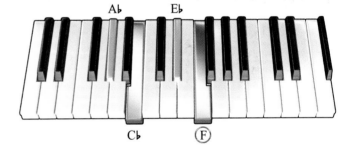

Ab   Eb

Cb   (F)

F minor7b5 (second inversion)

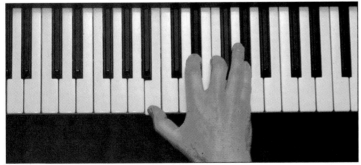

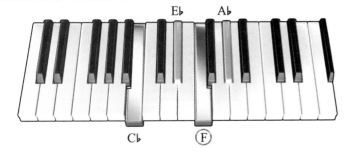

Eb   Ab

Cb   (F)

F minor7b5 (third inversion)

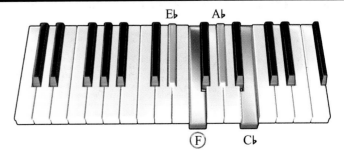

Eb   Ab

(F)   Cb

F

F minor (major7)

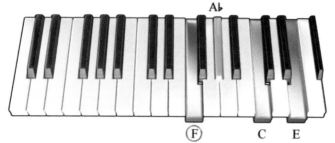

A♭

F   C   E

F minor (major7) *(first inversion)*

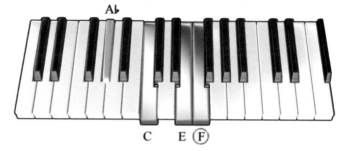

A♭

C   E F

F minor (major7) *(second inversion)*

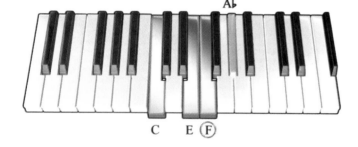

A♭

C   E F

F minor (major7) *(third inversion)*

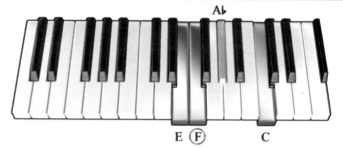

A♭

E F   C

F chords
using both hands

F7♭9

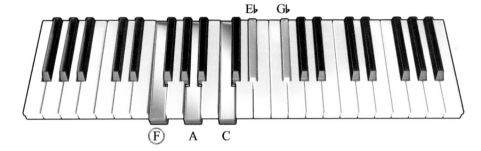

E♭   G♭

Ⓕ   A   C

F7♯9

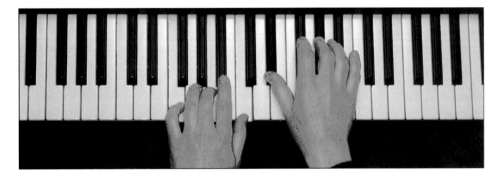

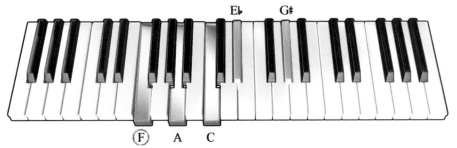

E♭   G♯

Ⓕ   A   C

F9

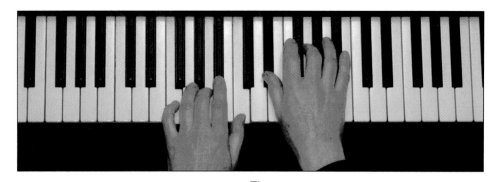

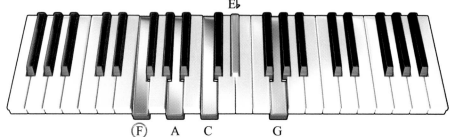

F9sus4

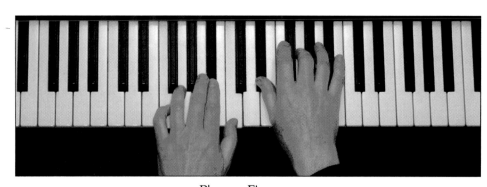

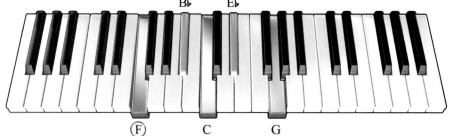

F9♭5

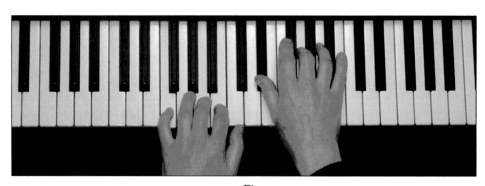

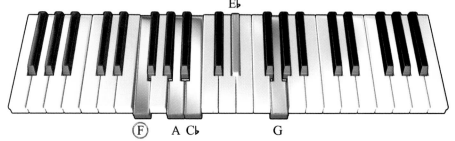

F9#5

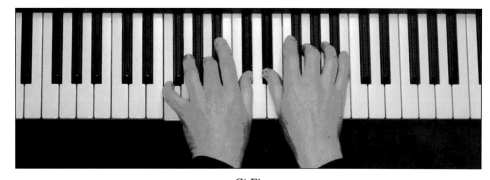

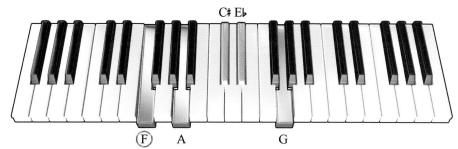

C# Eb

Ⓕ   A   G

F9#11

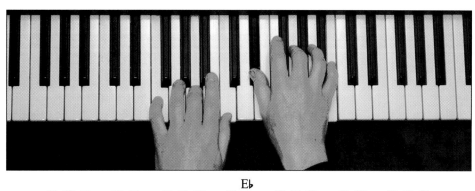

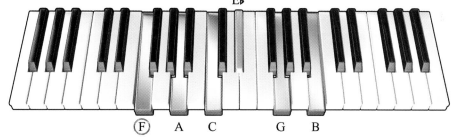

Eb

Ⓕ A C   G B

F13

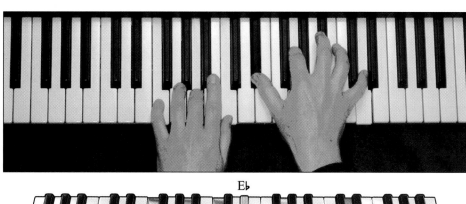

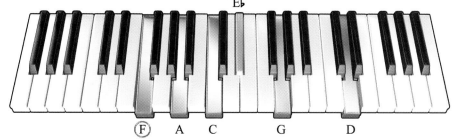

Eb

Ⓕ A C   G   D

F

F13sus4

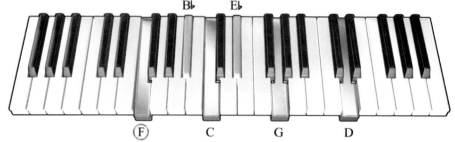

F13♭5

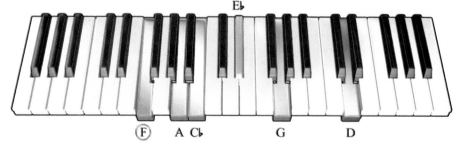

F13♯5

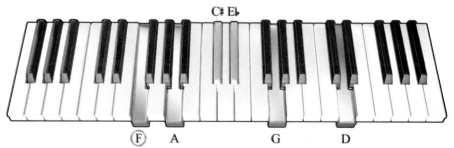

F13♭9

E♭   G♭

Ⓕ   A   C   D

F13♯9

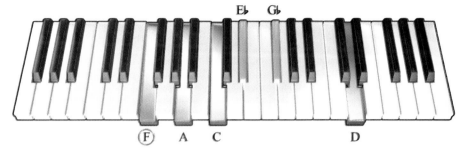

E♭   G♯

Ⓕ   A   C   D

F13♭5♭9

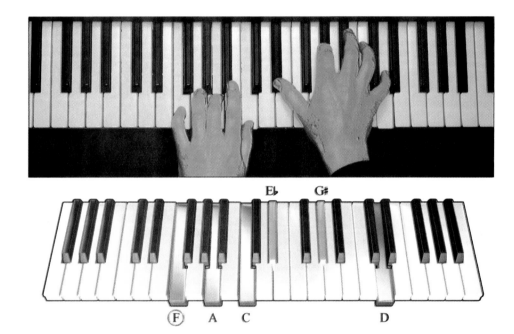

E♭   G♭

Ⓕ   A C♭   D

F

F13b5#9

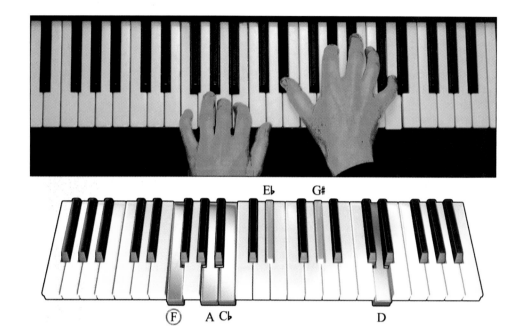

Eb   G#

F   A Cb   D

F13#5b9

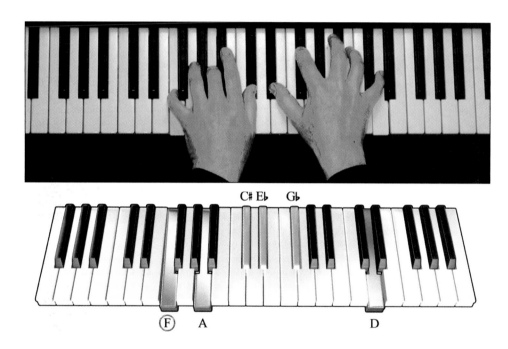

C# Eb   Gb

F   A   D

F13#5#9

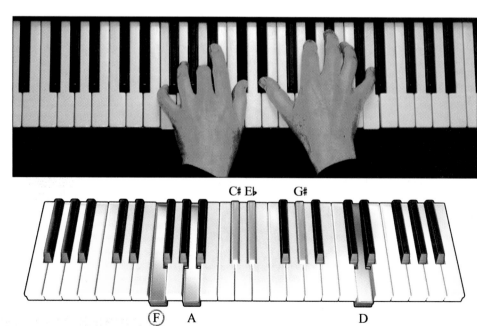

C# Eb   G#

F   A   D

F 6/9

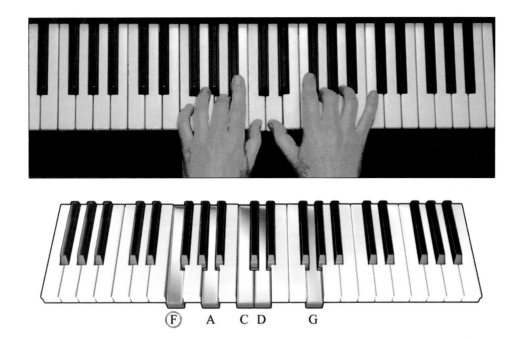

F   A   C D   G

F major9

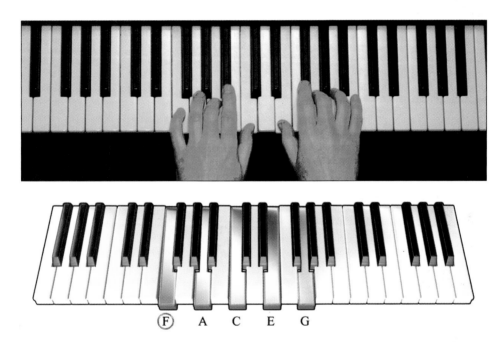

F   A   C   E   G

F major9#11

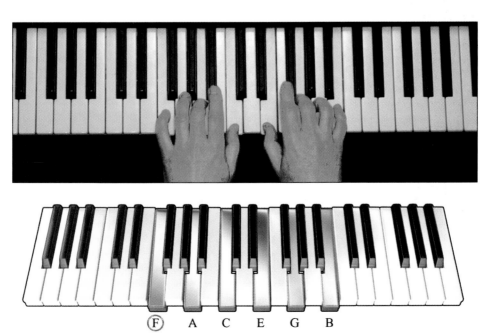

F   A   C   E   G   B

F

F major13

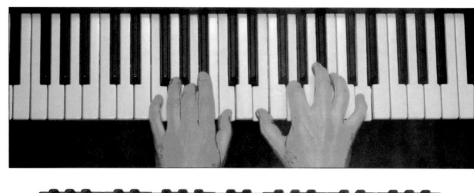

Ⓕ   A   C   E   G   D

F major13b5

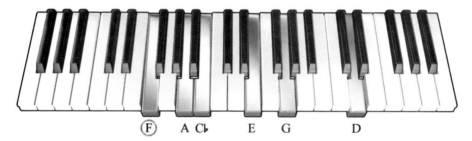

Ⓕ   A Cb   E   G   D

F major13#5

C#

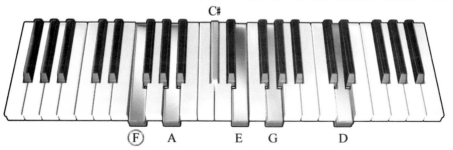

Ⓕ   A   E   G   D

F major13♭9

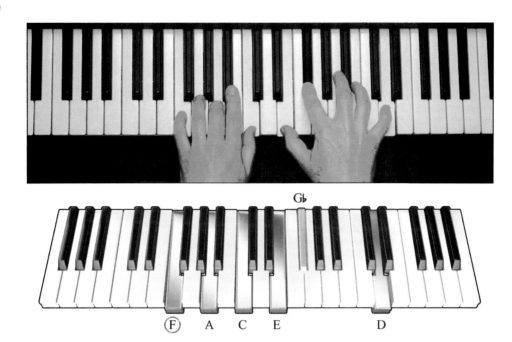

G♭

Ⓕ A C E D

F major13♯9

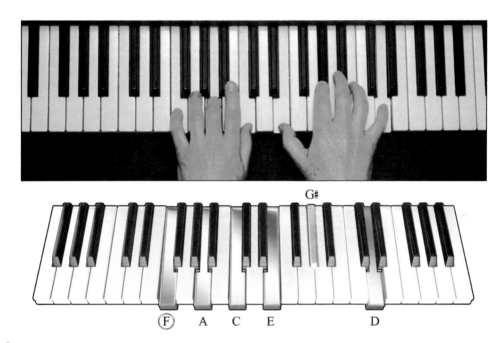

G♯

Ⓕ A C E D

F

F major13♭5♭9

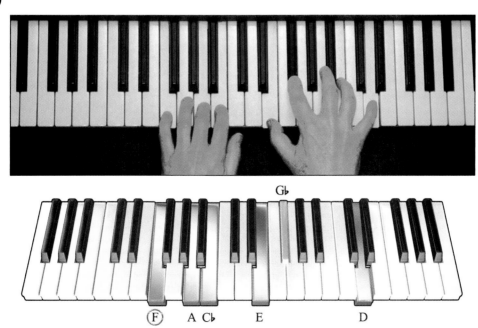

G♭

Ⓕ A C♭ E D

F major13♭5♯9

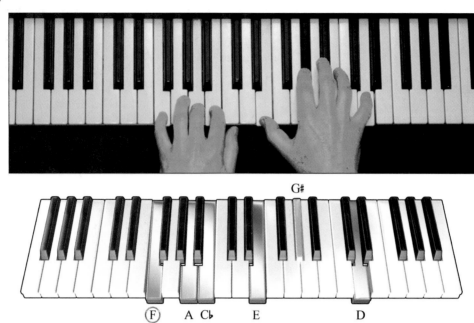

G#

(F) A C♭ E D

F major13♯5♭9

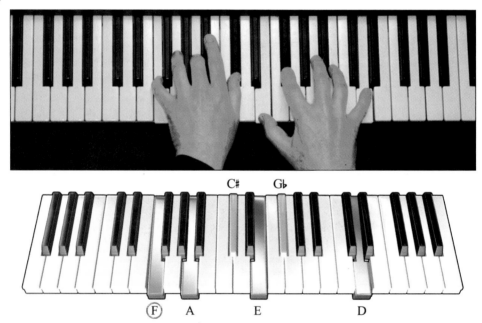

C# G♭

(F) A E D

F major13♯5♯9

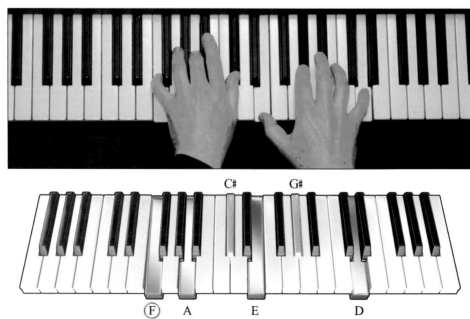

C# G#

(F) A E D

F minor7♭9

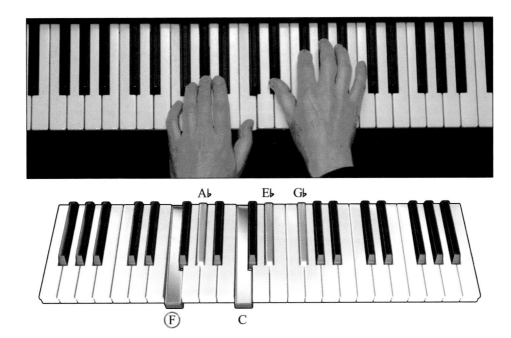

A♭ E♭ G♭

F C

F minor9

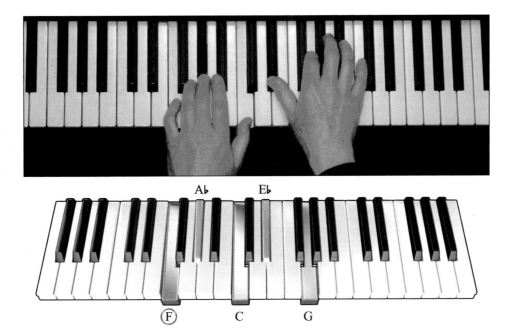

A♭ E♭

F C G

F minor11

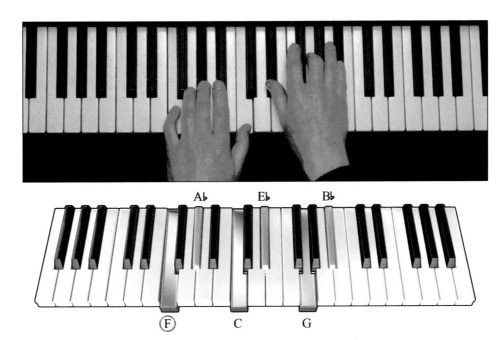

A♭ E♭ B♭

F C G

F

F minor13

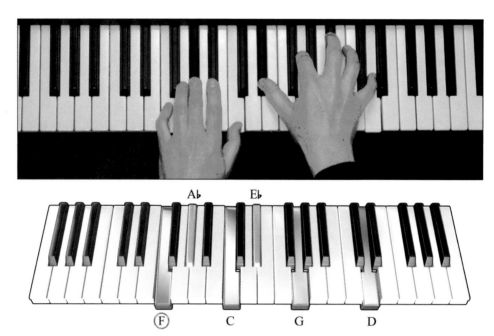

F minor9 (major7)

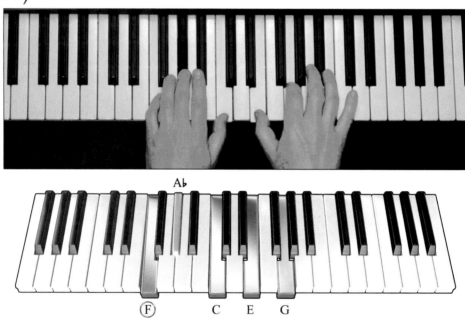

F# chords

F# major

F#/A# *(first inversion)*

F#/C# *(second inversion)*

F# augmented

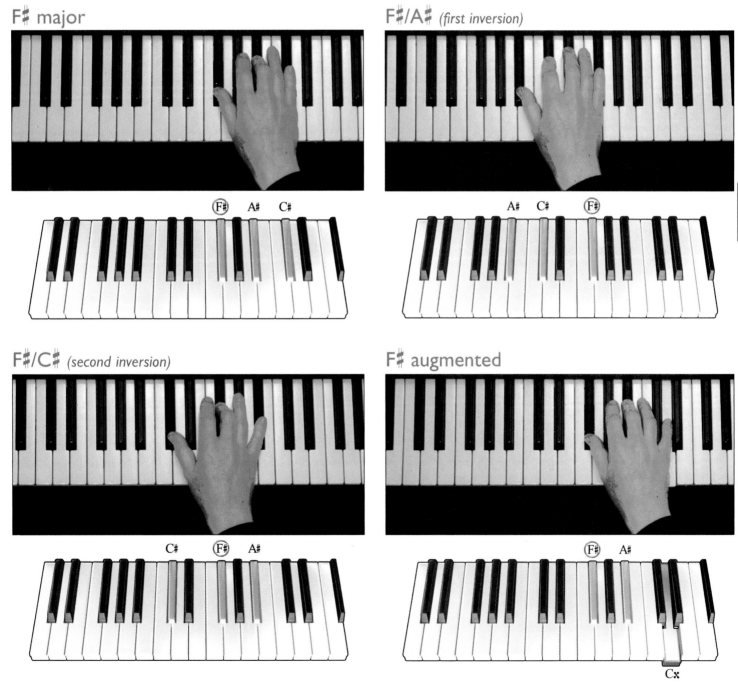

F#   A#   C#

A#   C#   (F#)

C#   (F#)   A#

(F#)   A#

Cx

F# augmented (first inversion)

A#   (F#)

Cx

F# augmented (second inversion)

(F#)   A#

Cx

F#sus4

(F#)   C#

B

F#sus4 (first inversion)

C#   (F#)

B

F#sus4 (second inversion)

C#   (F#)

B

F#6

(F#)   A#   C# D#

F#6 *(first inversion)*

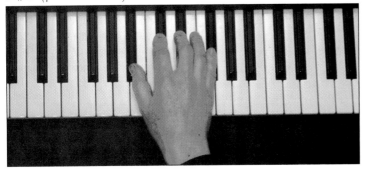

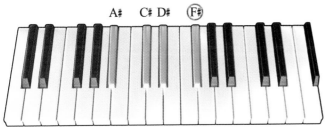

A# C# D# (F#)

F#6 *(second inversion)*

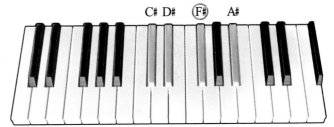

C# D# (F#) A#

F#6 *(third inversion)*

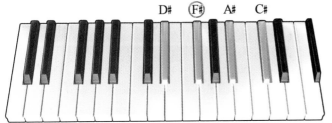

D# (F#) A# C#

F#7

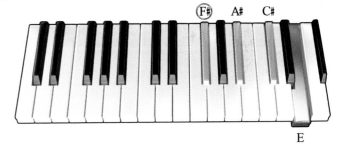

(F#) A# C#

E

F#7 *(first inversion)*

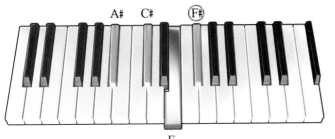

A# C# (F#)

E

F#7 *(second inversion)*

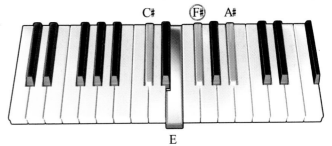

C# (F#) A#

E

F#7 (third inversion)

F#   A#   C#

E

F#°7

F#   Eb

A   C

F#°7 (first inversion)

Eb   F#

A   C

F#°7 (second inversion)

Eb   F#

C   A

F#°7 (third inversion)

Eb   F#

A   C

F# major7

F#   A#   C#

E#

F# major7 *(first inversion)*

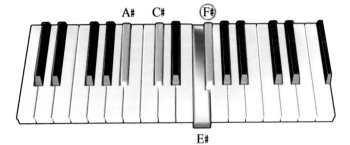

A#　C#　(F#)

E#

F# major7 *(second inversion)*

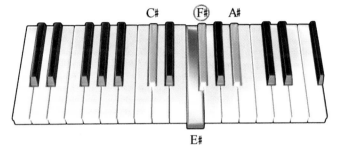

C#　(F#)　A#

E#

F# major7 *(third inversion)*

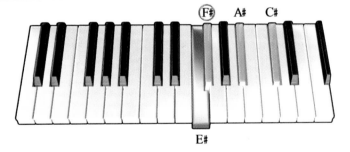

(F#)　A#　C#

E#

F# minor

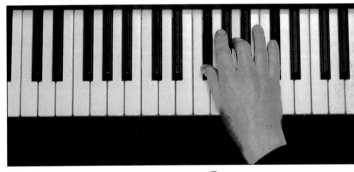

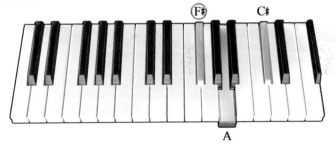

(F#)　C#

A

F# minor *(first inversion)*

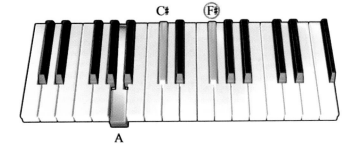

C#　(F#)

A

F# minor *(second inversion)*

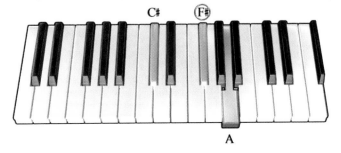

C#　(F#)

A

F#

F# minor6

F#   C# D#

A

F# minor6 *(first inversion)*

C# D#   F#

A

F# minor6 *(second inversion)*

C# D#   F#

A

F# minor6 *(third inversion)*

D#   F#   C#

A

F# minor7

F#   C#

A   E

F# minor7 *(first inversion)*

C#   F#

A   E

F♯ minor7 (second inversion)

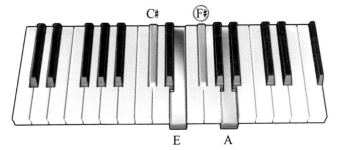

C♯ (F♯)

E   A

F♯ minor7 (third inversion)

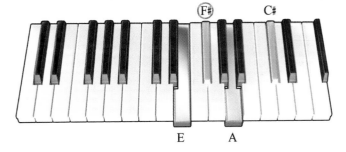

(F♯)   C♯

E   A

F♯ minor7♭5

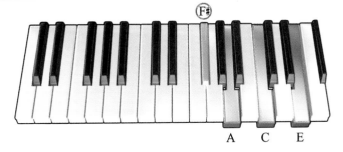

(F♯)

A   C   E

F♯ minor7♭5 (first inversion)

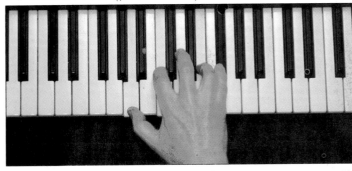

(F♯)

A   C   E

F♯ minor7♭5 (second inversion)

(F♯)

C   E   A

F♯ minor7♭5 (third inversion)

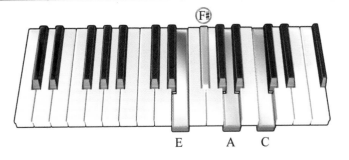

(F♯)

E   A   C

F♯

F# minor (major7)

F#   C#

A   E#

F# minor (major7) *(first inversion)*

C#   F#

A   E#

F# minor (major7) *(second inversion)*

C#   F#

E#   A

F# minor (major7) *(third inversion)*

F#   C#

E#   A

F# chords
using both hands

F#7♭9

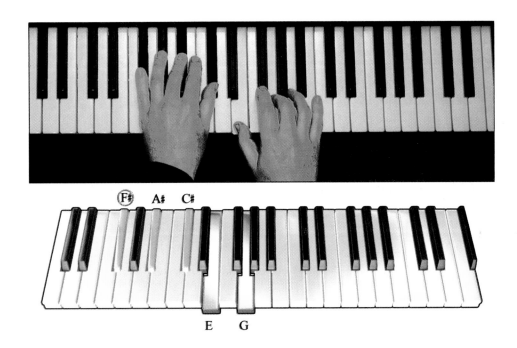

F#7#9

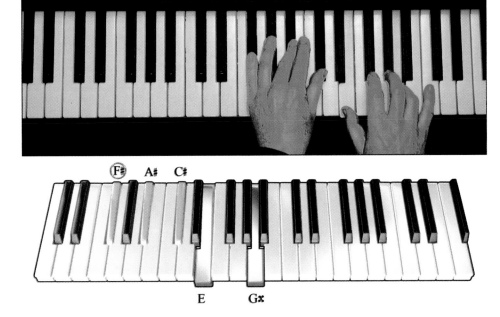

F#9

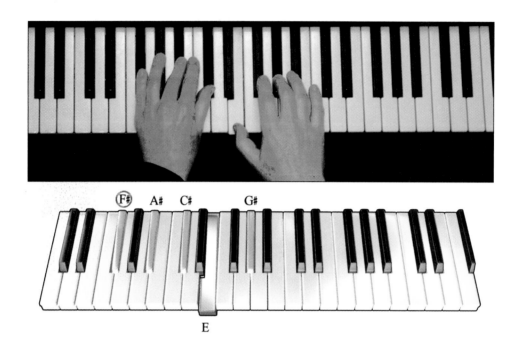

F#   A#   C#   G#

E

F#9sus4

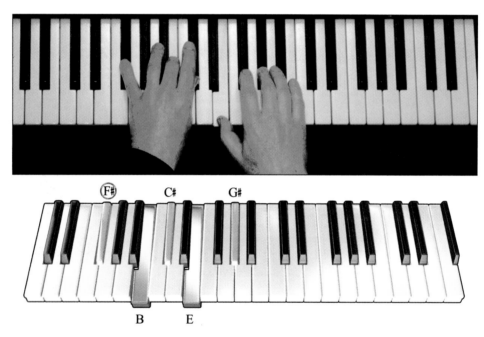

F#   C#   G#

B   E

F#9♭5

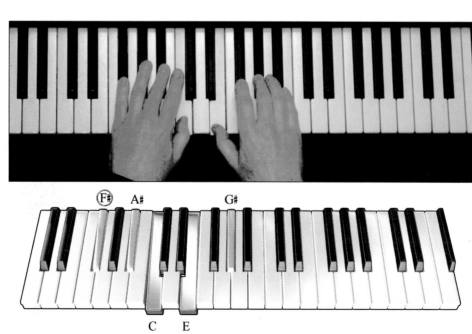

F#   A#   G#

C   E

F#9#5

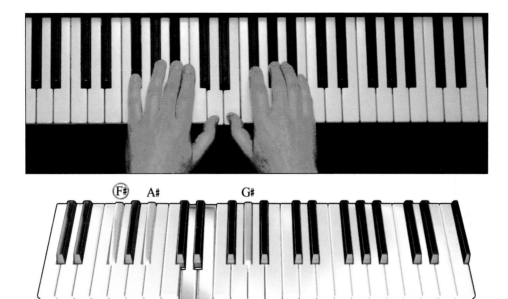

F#   A#   G#

Cx E

F#9#11

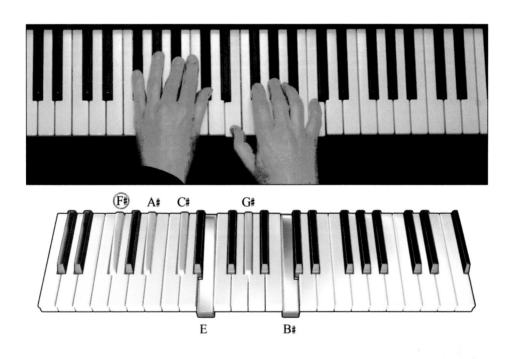

F#   A#   C#   G#

E   B#

F#13

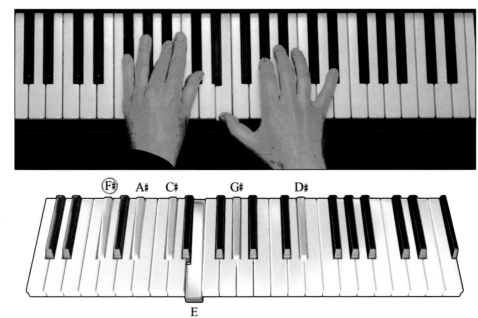

F#   A#   C#   G#   D#

E

F#13sus4

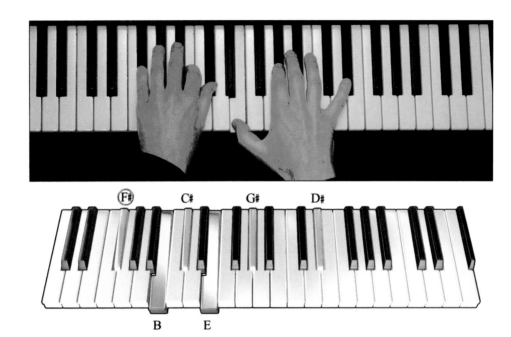

F#   C#   G#   D#

B   E

F#13♭5

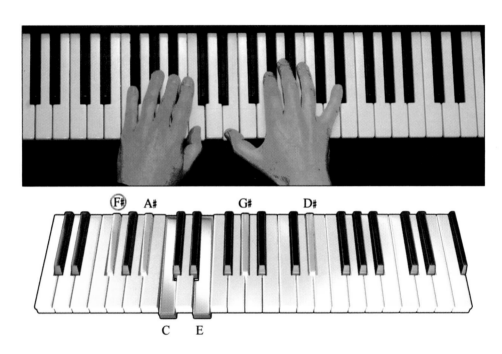

F#   A#   G#   D#

C   E

F#13#5

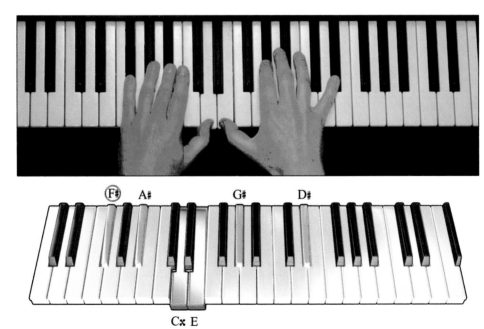

F#   A#   G#   D#

C𝄪 E

F#13♭9

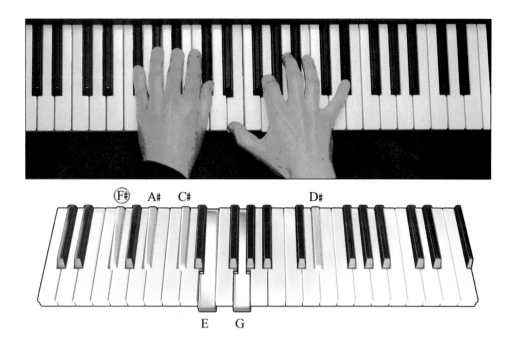

F#13#9

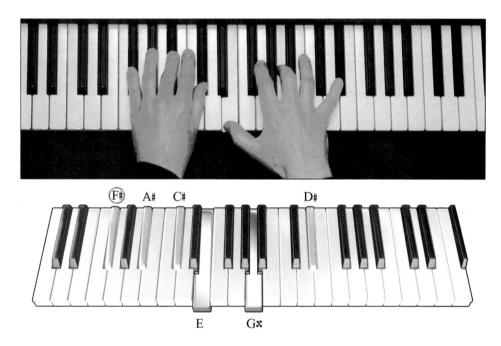

F#13♭5♭9

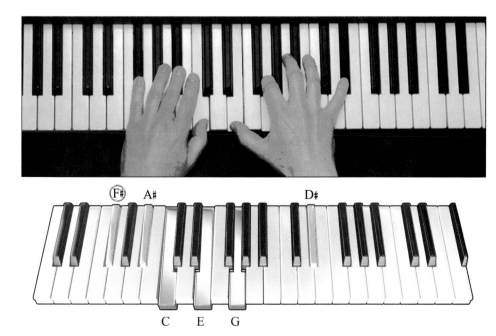

F#13♭5#9

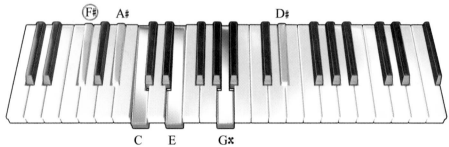

F#13#5♭9

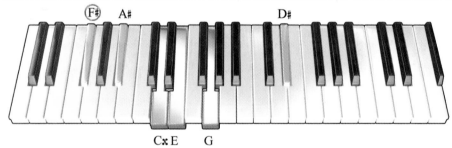

F#13#5#9

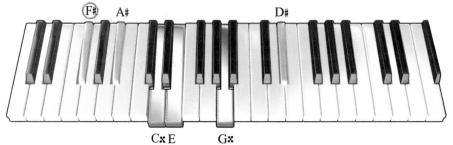

F# 6/9

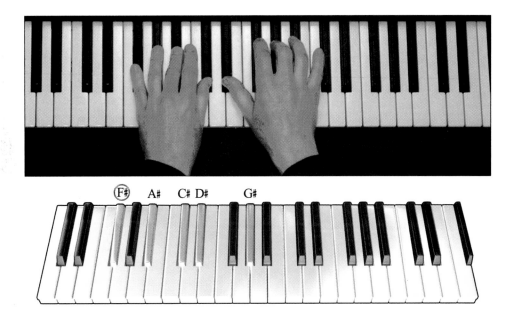

(F#)　A#　C# D#　　G#

F# major9

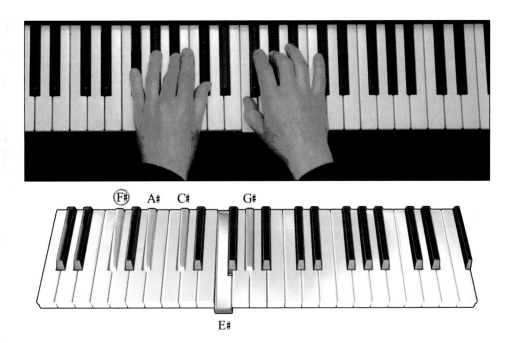

(F#)　A#　C#　　G#

E#

F# major9#11

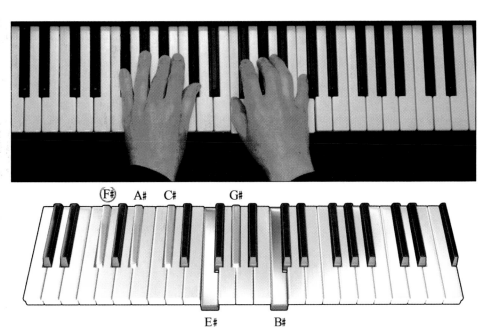

(F#)　A#　C#　　G#

E#　　　　B#

F#

F# major13

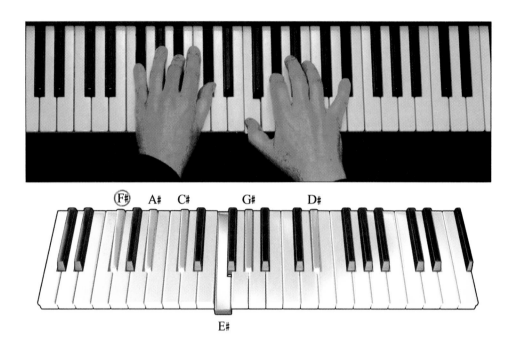

F#   A#   C#   G#   D#

E#

F# major13♭5

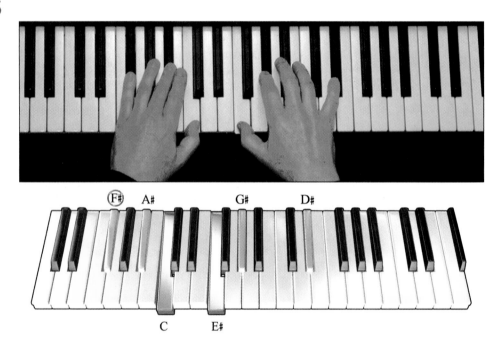

F#   A#   G#   D#

C   E#

F# major13#5

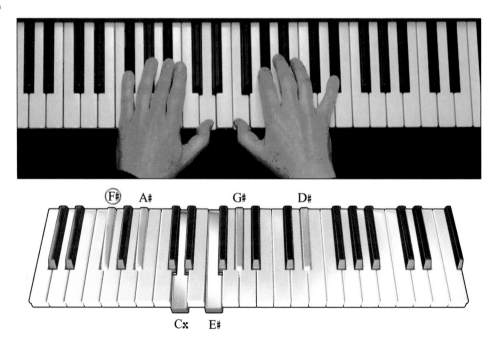

F#   A#   G#   D#

Cx   E#

F# major13♭9

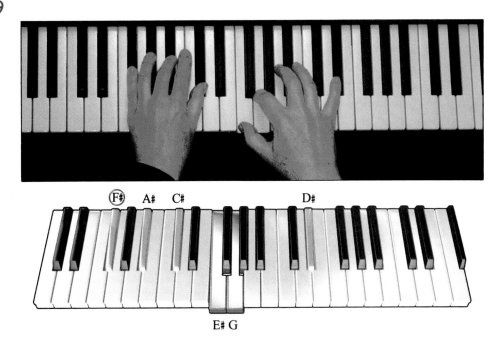

F# A# C# D#

E# G

F# major13#9

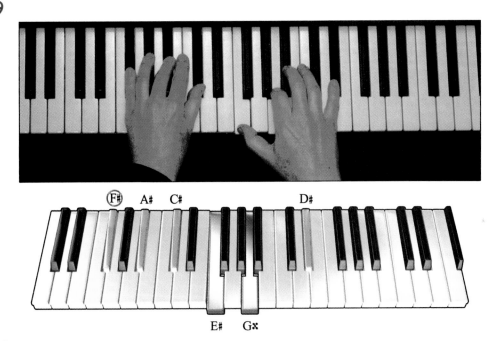

F# A# C# D#

E# G𝄪

F# major13♭5♭9

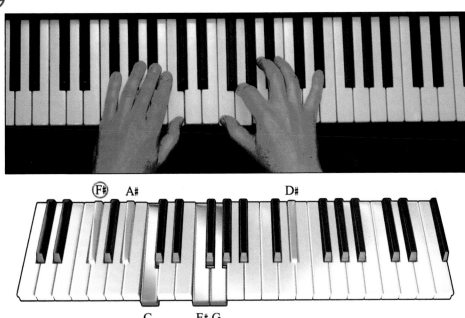

F# A# D#

C E# G

F#

F# major13♭5#9

F# major13#5♭9

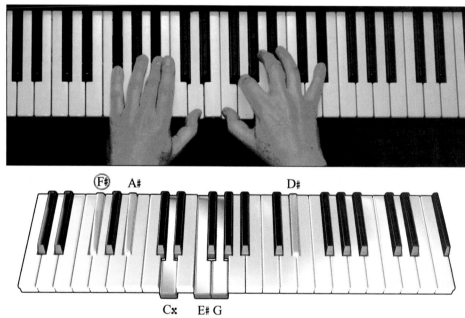

F# major13#5#9

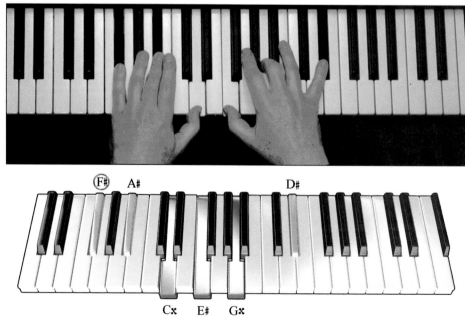

F♯ minor7♭9

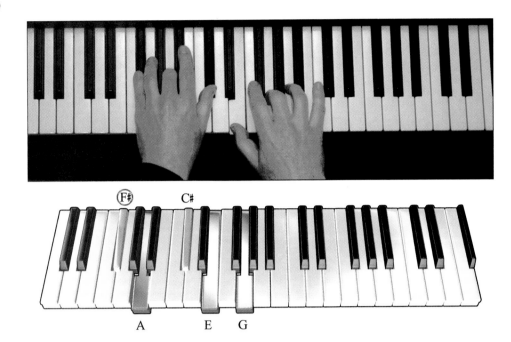

F♯   C♯

A   E   G

F♯ minor9

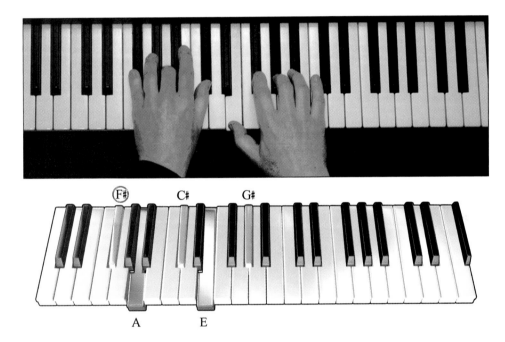

F♯   C♯   G♯

A   E

F♯ minor11

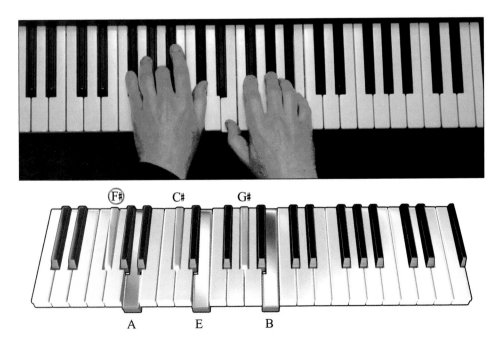

F♯   C♯   G♯

A   E   B

F♯ minor13

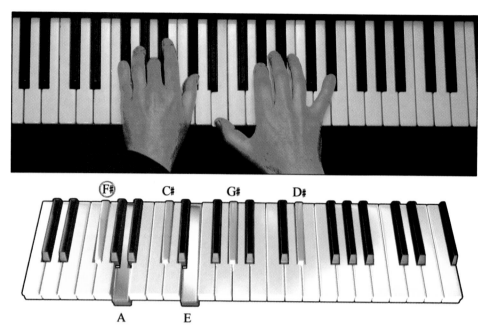

F♯ minor9 (major7)

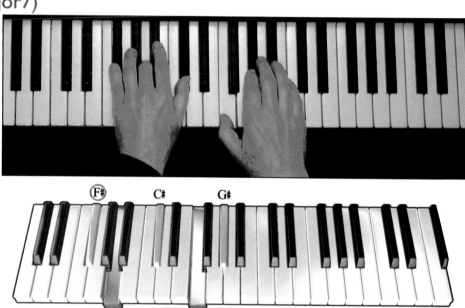

G chords

G major

G/B *(first inversion)*

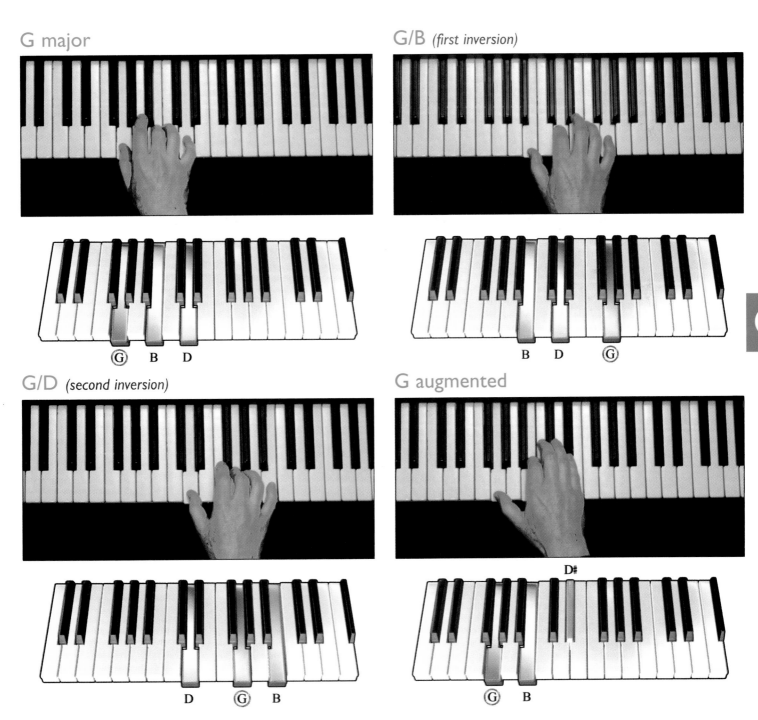

Ⓖ B D

B D Ⓖ

G/D *(second inversion)*

G augmented

D#

D Ⓖ B

Ⓖ B

G

G augmented (first inversion)

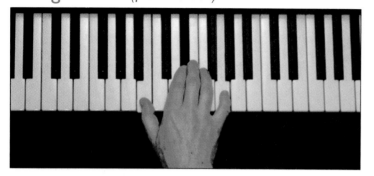

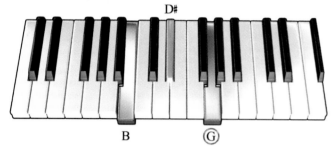

B   Ⓖ   D#

G augmented (second inversion)

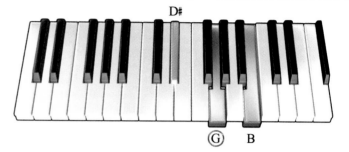

D#   Ⓖ   B

Gsus4

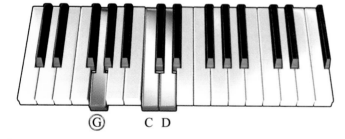

Ⓖ   C D

Gsus4 (first inversion)

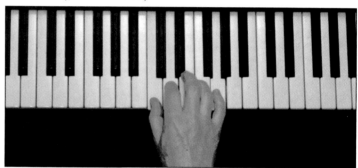

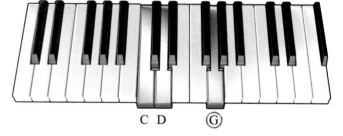

C D   Ⓖ

Gsus4 (second inversion)

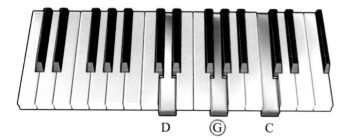

D   Ⓖ   C

G6

Ⓖ   B   D E

G6 (first inversion)

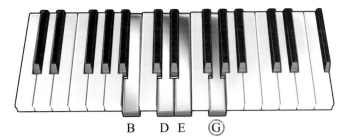

B   D   E   Ⓖ

G6 (second inversion)

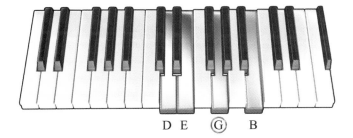

D   E   Ⓖ   B

G6 (third inversion)

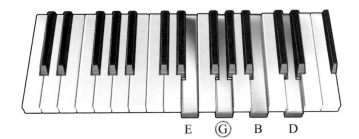

E   Ⓖ   B   D

G7

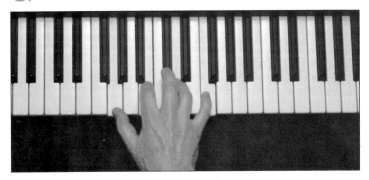

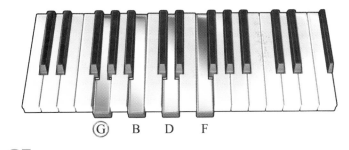

Ⓖ   B   D   F

G7 (first inversion)

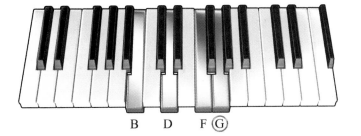

B   D   F Ⓖ

G7 (second inversion)

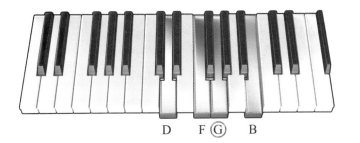

D   F Ⓖ   B

G

G7 (third inversion)

F ⒢ B D

G°7

B♭ D♭

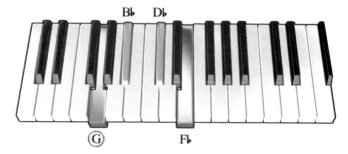

⒢ F♭

G°7 (first inversion)

B♭ D♭

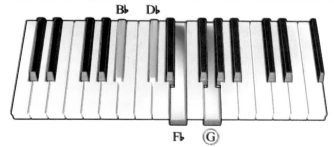

F♭ ⒢

G°7 (second inversion)

D♭ B♭

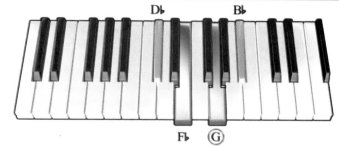

F♭ ⒢

G°7 (third inversion)

B♭ D♭

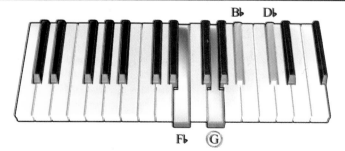

F♭ ⒢

G major7

F#

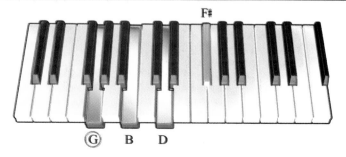

⒢ B D

G major7 (first inversion)

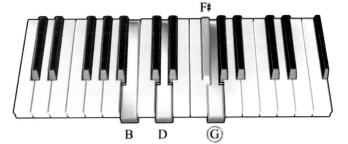

F#

B   D   (G)

G major7 (second inversion)

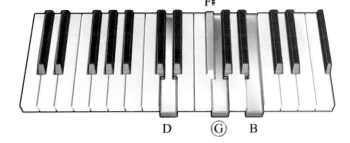

F#

D   (G)   B

G major7 (third inversion)

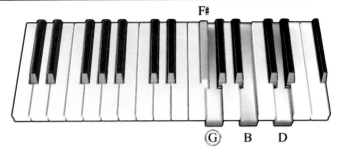

F#

(G)   B   D

G minor

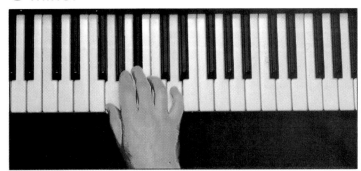

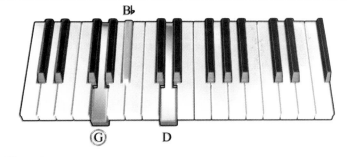

B♭

(G)   D

G minor (first inversion)

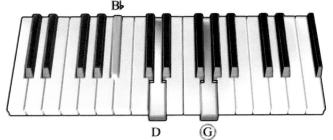

B♭

D   (G)

G minor (second inversion)

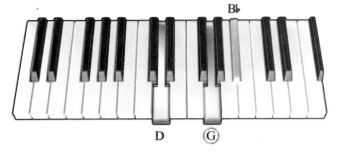

B♭

D   (G)

G

G minor6

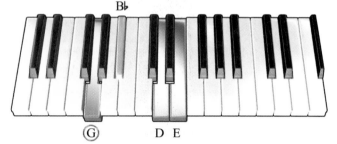

B♭

G D E

G minor6 *(first inversion)*

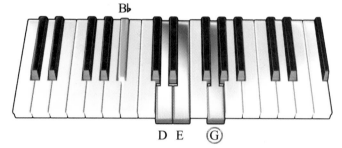

B♭

D E G

G minor6 *(second inversion)*

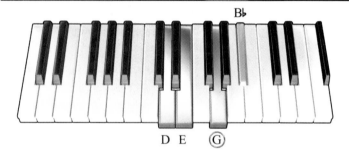

B♭

D E G

G minor6 *(third inversion)*

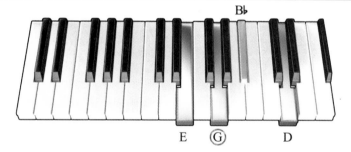

B♭

E G D

G minor7

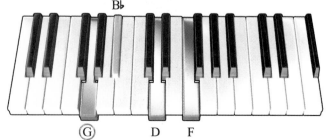

B♭

G D F

G minor7 *(first inversion)*

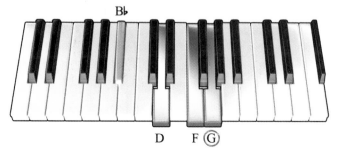

B♭

D F G

G minor7 *(second inversion)*

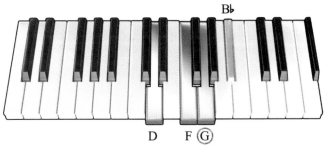

Bb

D   F G

G minor7 *(third inversion)*

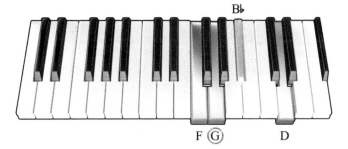

Bb

F G   D

G minor7b5

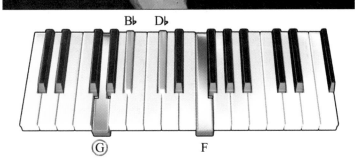

Bb   Db

G   F

G minor7b5 *(first inversion)*

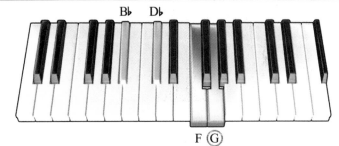

Bb   Db

F G

G minor7b5 *(second inversion)*

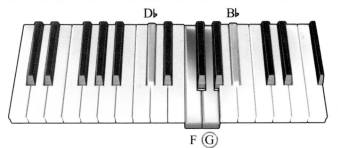

Db   Bb

F G

G minor7b5 *(third inversion)*

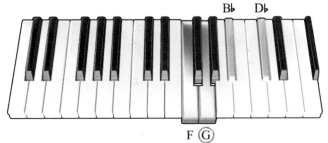

Bb   Db

F G

G

G minor (major7)

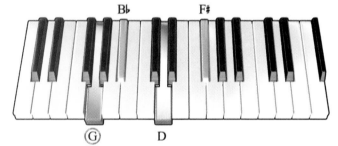

B♭   F#

G   D

G minor (major7) *(first inversion)*

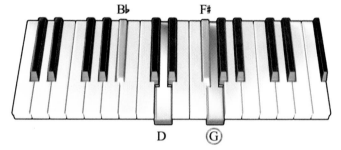

B♭   F#

D   G

G minor (major7) *(second inversion)*

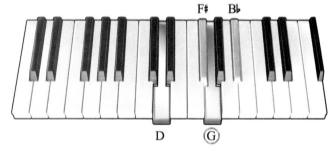

F#   B♭

D   G

G minor (major7) *(third inversion)*

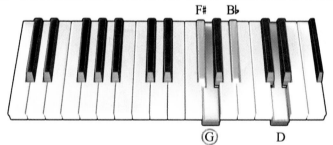

F#   B♭

G   D

G chords
using both hands

G7♭9

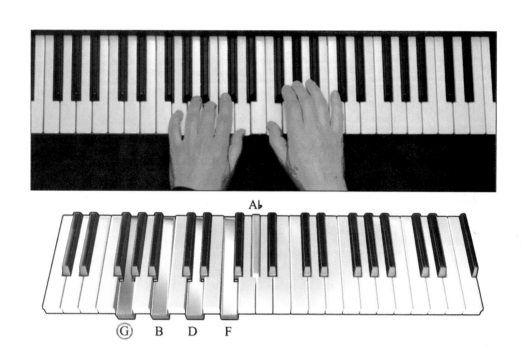

A♭

Ⓖ B D F

G7♯9

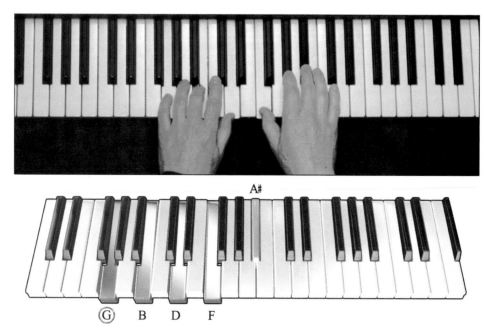

A♯

Ⓖ B D F

159

G

G9

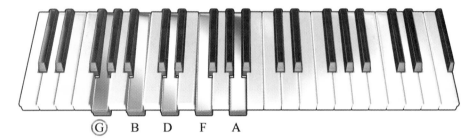

Ⓖ   B   D   F   A

G9sus4

Ⓖ   C D   F   A

G9♭5

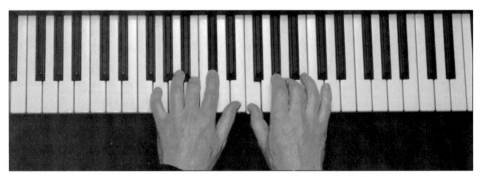

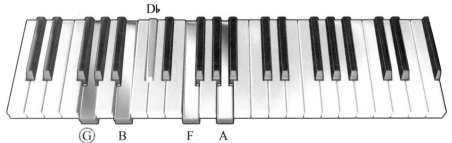

D♭

Ⓖ   B   F   A

G9#5

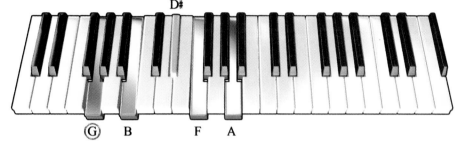

D#

Ⓖ B F A

G9#11

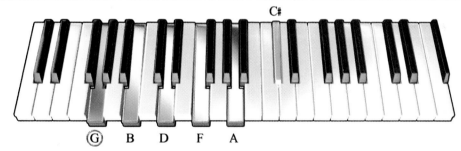

C#

Ⓖ B D F A

G13

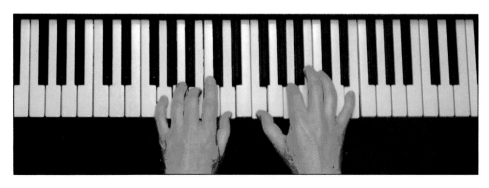

Ⓖ B D F A E

G

G13sus4

Ⓖ   C D   F   A   E

G13♭5

D♭

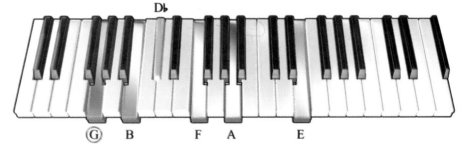

Ⓖ   B   F   A   E

G13♯5

D♯

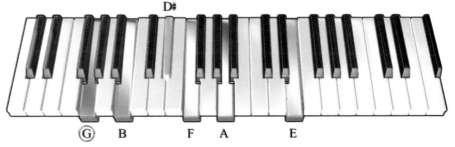

Ⓖ   B   F   A   E

G13♭9

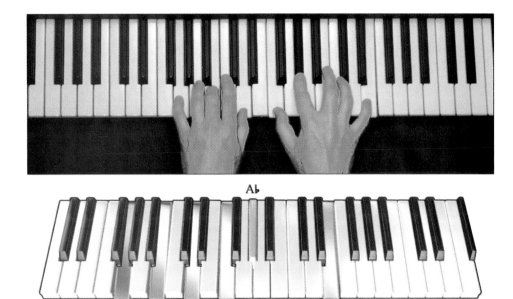

G13♯9

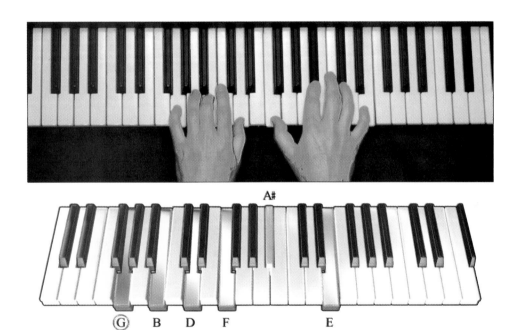

G13♭5♭9

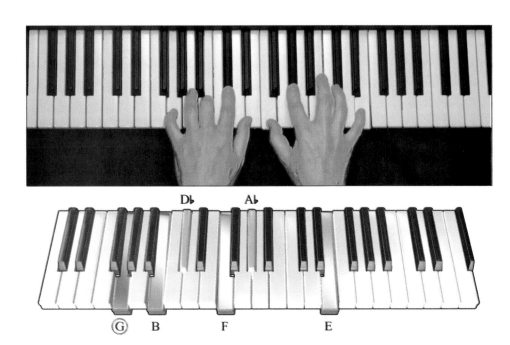

G

G13b5#9

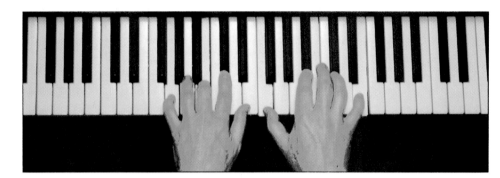

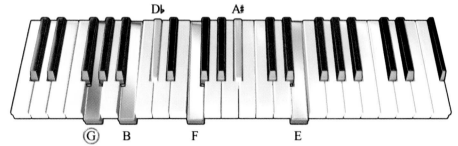

D♭ A#

G B F E

G13#5b9

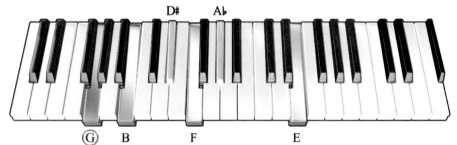

D# A♭

G B F E

G13#5#9

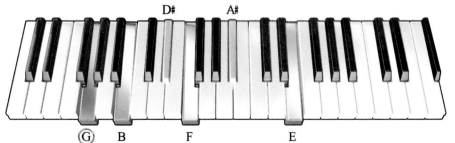

D# A#

G B F E

G 6/9

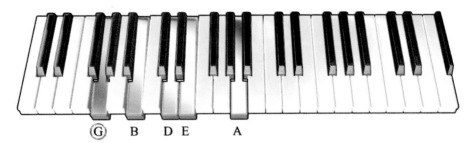

Ⓖ   B   D E   A

G major9

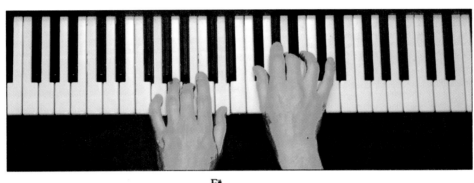

F#

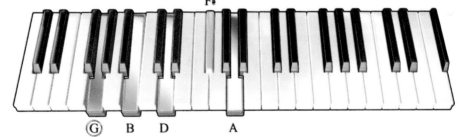

Ⓖ   B   D   A

G major9#11

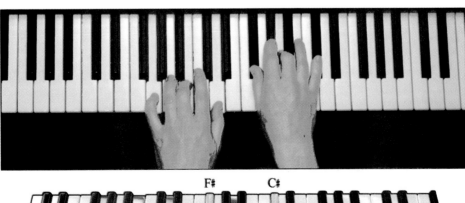

F#   C#

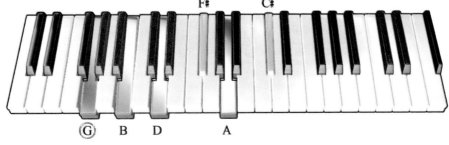

Ⓖ   B   D   A

G

G major13

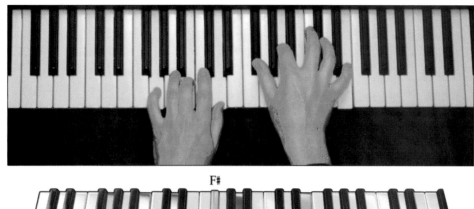

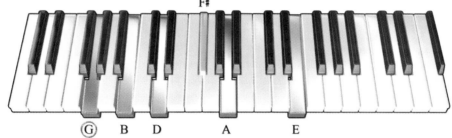

F#

Ⓖ B D   A   E

G major13♭5

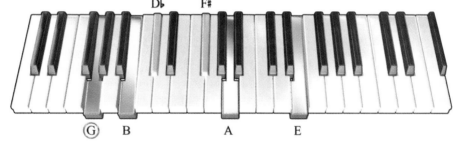

D♭   F#

Ⓖ B   A   E

G major13♯5

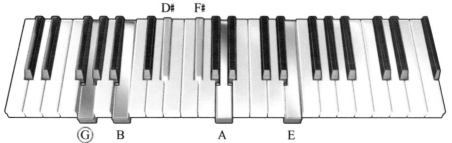

D#   F#

Ⓖ B   A   E

G major13♭9

F# A♭

Ⓖ   B   D   E

G major13♯9

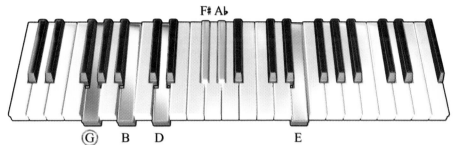

F#   A#

Ⓖ   B   D   E

G major13♭5♭9

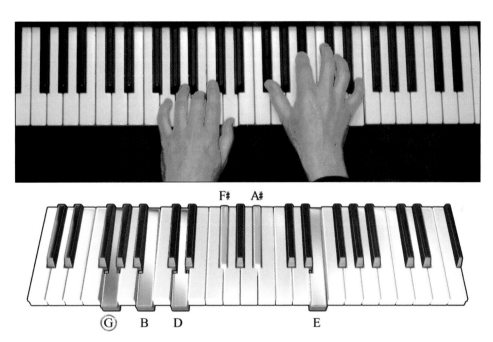

D♭   F# A♭

Ⓖ   B   E

G

G major13♭5♯9

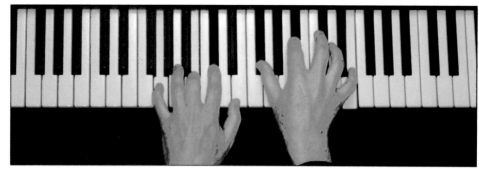

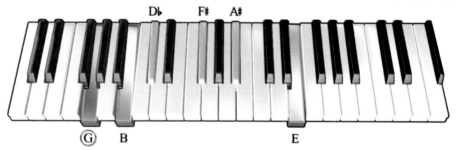

D♭   F♯   A♯

Ⓖ   B   E

G major13♯5♭9

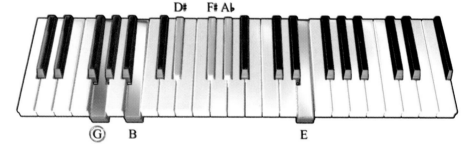

D♯   F♯ A♭

Ⓖ   B   E

G major13♯5♯9

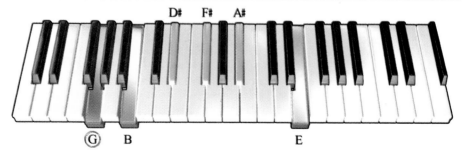

D♯   F♯   A♯

Ⓖ   B   E

G minor7♭9

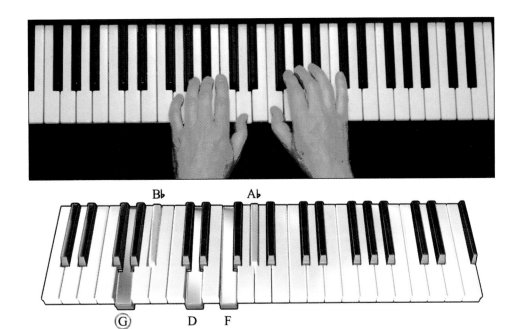

G minor9

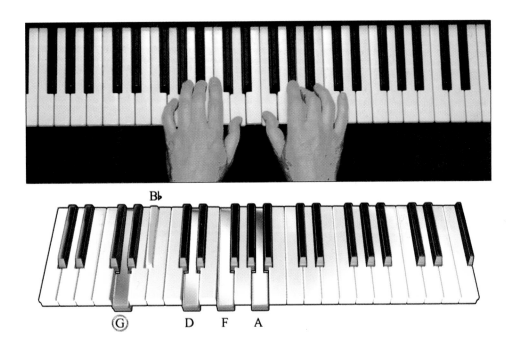

G minor11

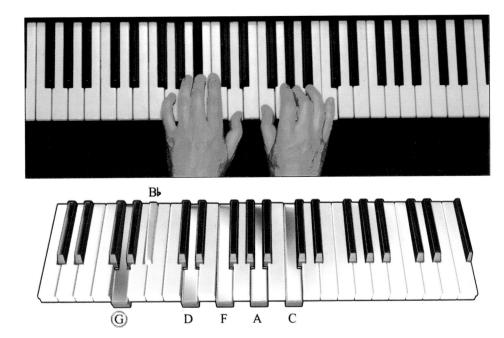

G

G minor13

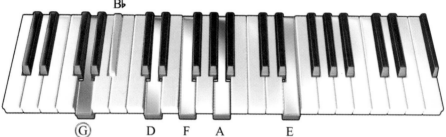

B♭

Ⓖ   D   F   A   E

G minor9 (major7)

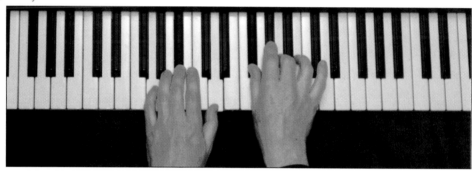

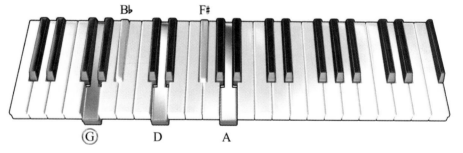

B♭   F#

Ⓖ   D   A

A♭ chords

A♭ major

A♭/C (first inversion)

A♭/E♭ (second inversion)

A♭ augmented

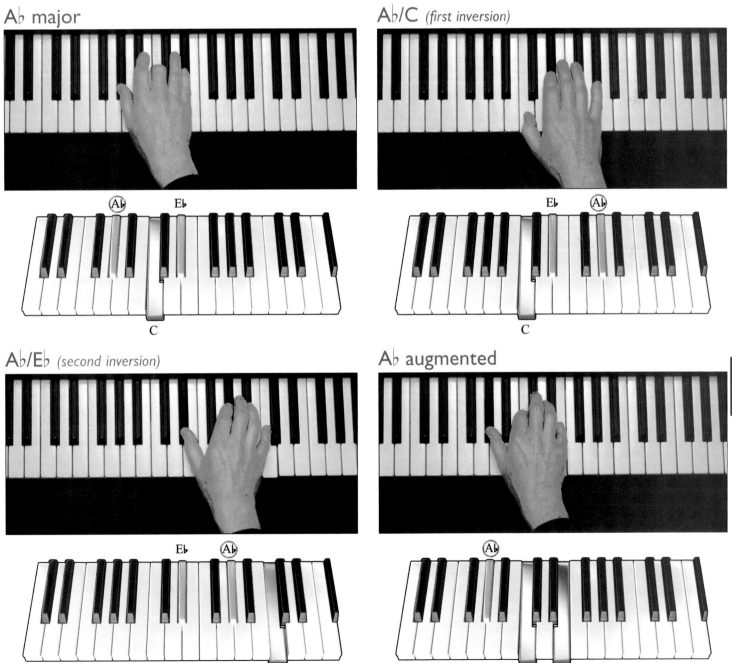

A♭ augmented *(first inversion)*

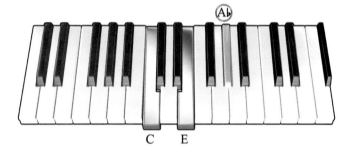

Ⓐ♭

C E

A♭sus4

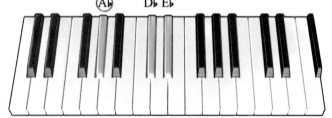

Ⓐ♭ D♭ E♭

A♭sus4 *(second inversion)*

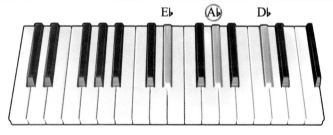

E♭ Ⓐ♭ D♭

A♭ augmented *(second inversion)*

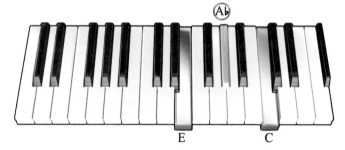

Ⓐ♭

E C

A♭sus4 *(first inversion)*

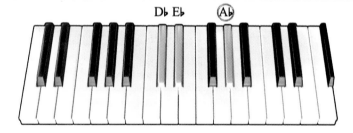

D♭ E♭ Ⓐ♭

A♭6

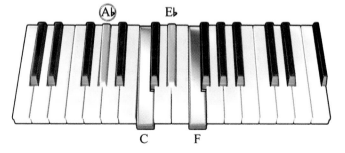

Ⓐ♭ E♭

C F

A♭6 (first inversion)

A♭6 (second inversion)

A♭6 (third inversion)

A♭7

A♭7 (first inversion)

A♭7 (second inversion)

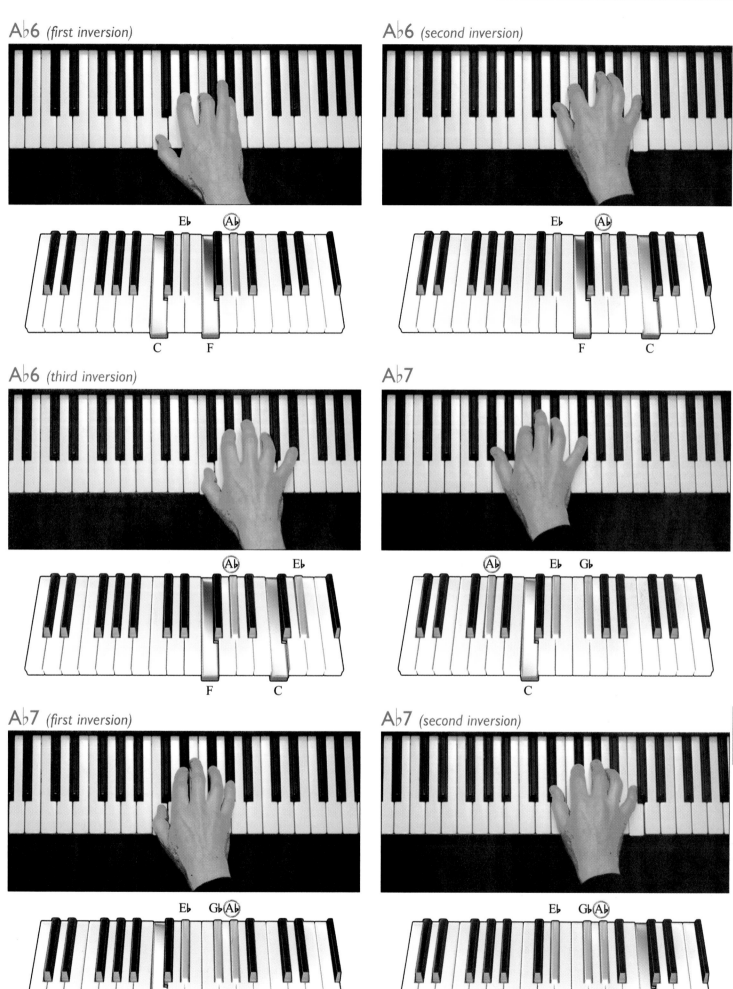

A♭

A♭7 (third inversion)

G♭ (A♭)   E♭

C

A♭°7

(A♭)

C♭   E♭♭   G♭♭

A♭°7 (first inversion)

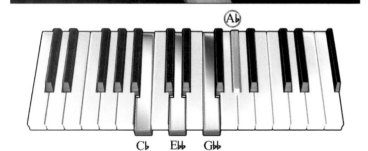

(A♭)

C♭   E♭♭   G♭♭

A♭°7 (second inversion)

(A♭)

E♭♭   G♭♭   C♭

A♭°7 (third inversion)

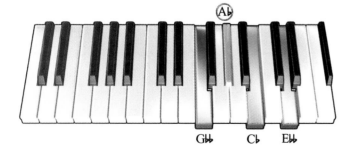

(A♭)

G♭♭   C♭   E♭♭

A♭ major7

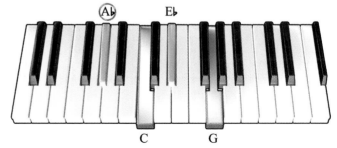

(A♭)   E♭

C   G

A♭ major7 *(first inversion)*

A♭ major7 *(second inversion)*

A♭ major7 *(third inversion)*

A♭ minor

A♭ minor *(first inversion)*

A♭ minor *(second inversion)*

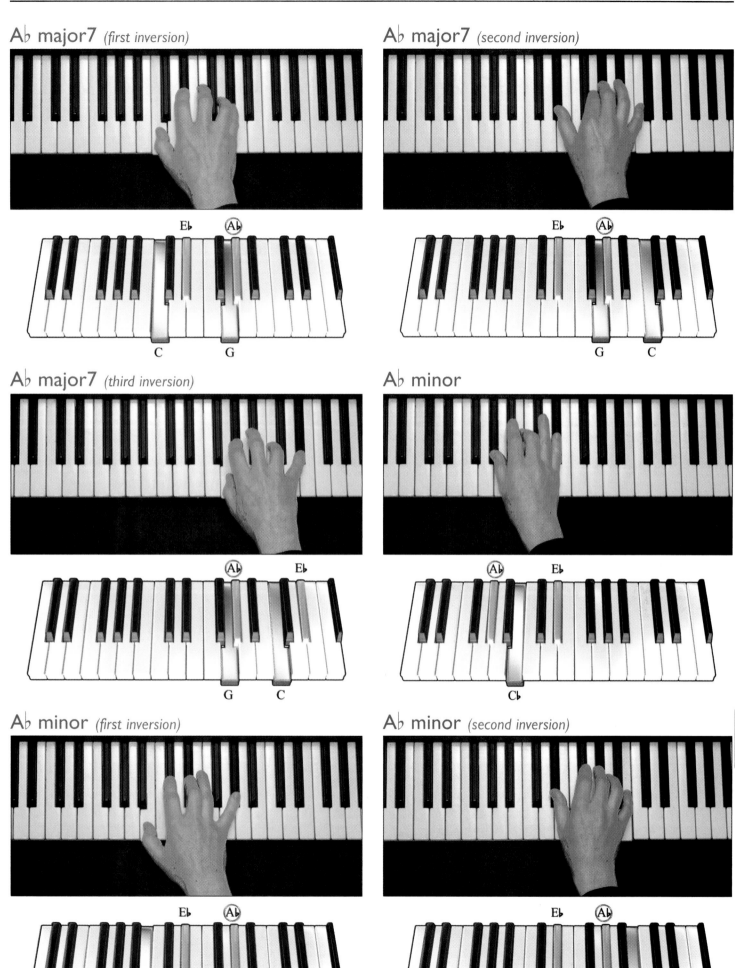

A♭

A♭ minor6

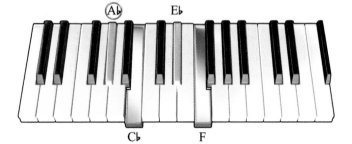

A♭   E♭

C♭   F

A♭ minor6 *(first inversion)*

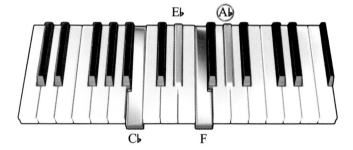

E♭   A♭

C♭   F

A♭ minor6 *(second inversion)*

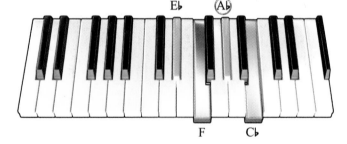

E♭   A♭

F   C♭

A♭ minor6 *(third inversion)*

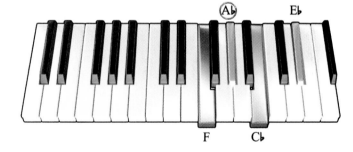

A♭   E♭

F   C♭

A♭ minor7

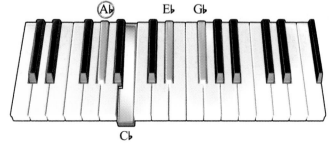

A♭   E♭   G♭

C♭

A♭ minor7 *(first inversion)*

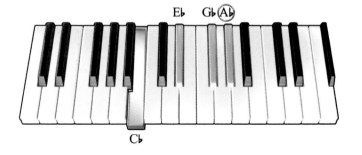

E♭   G♭ A♭

C♭

A♭ minor7 *(second inversion)*

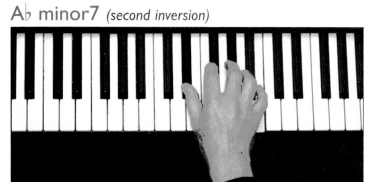

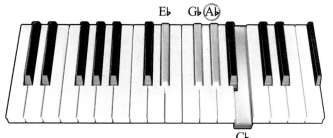

E♭ G♭ (A♭)

C♭

A♭ minor7 *(third inversion)*

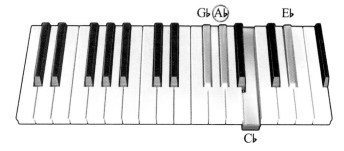

G♭ (A♭) E♭

C♭

A♭ minor7♭5

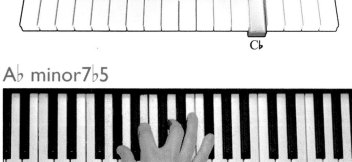

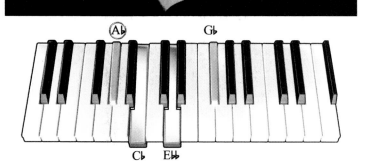

(A♭) G♭

C♭ E♭♭

A♭ minor7♭5 *(first inversion)*

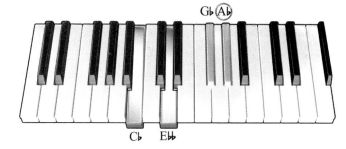

G♭ (A♭)

C♭ E♭♭

A♭ minor7♭5 *(second inversion)*

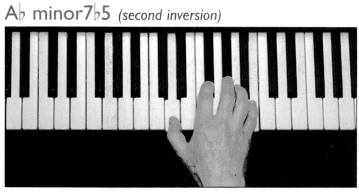

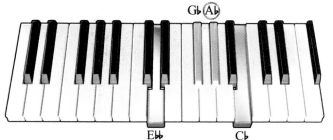

G♭ (A♭)

E♭♭ C♭

A♭ minor7♭5 *(third inversion)*

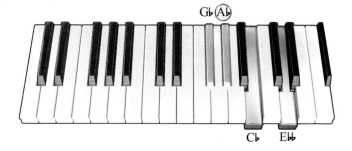

G♭ (A♭)

C♭ E♭♭

A♭

A♭ minor (major7)

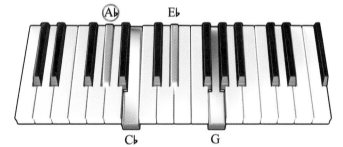

A♭   E♭

C♭   G

A♭ minor (major7) *(first inversion)*

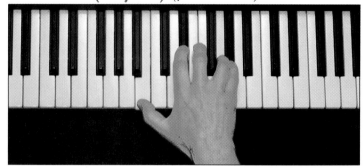

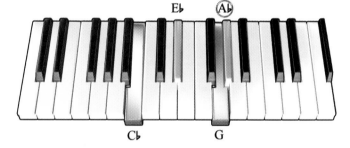

E♭   A♭

C♭   G

A♭ minor (major7) *(second inversion)*

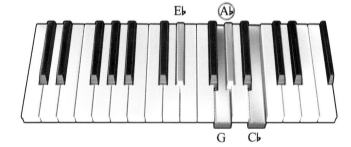

E♭   A♭

G   C♭

A♭ minor (major7) *(third inversion)*

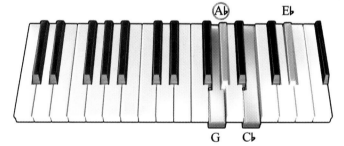

A♭   E♭

G   C♭

A♭ chords
using both hands

A♭7♭9

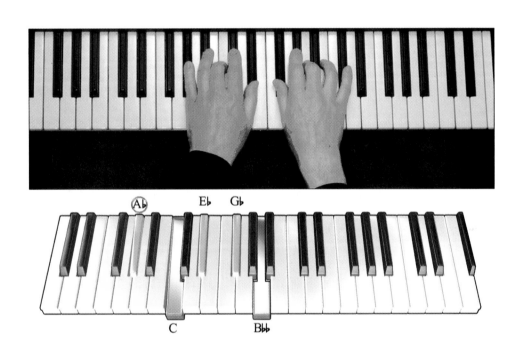

A♭7#9

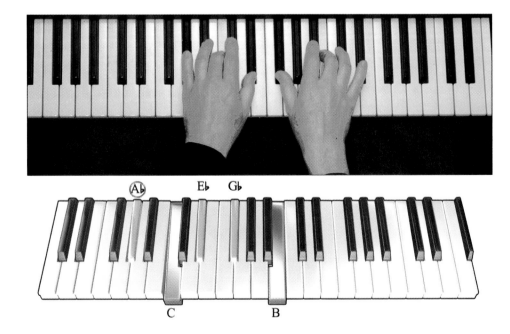

Ab9

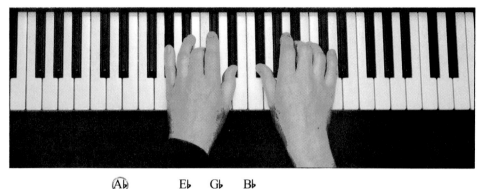

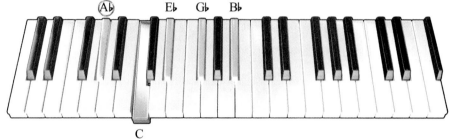

Ab9sus4

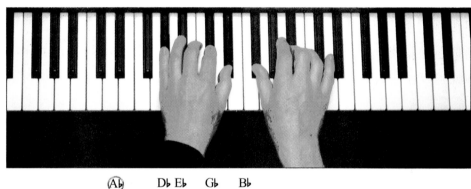

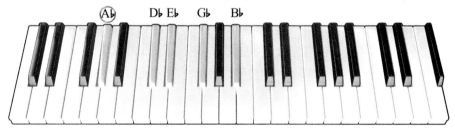

Ab9b5

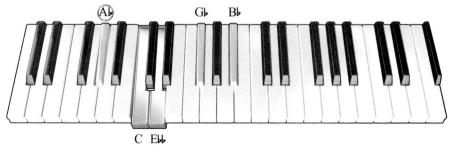

A♭9♯5

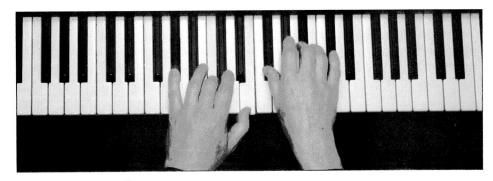

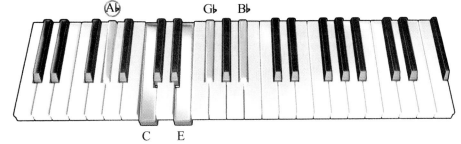

A♭9♯11

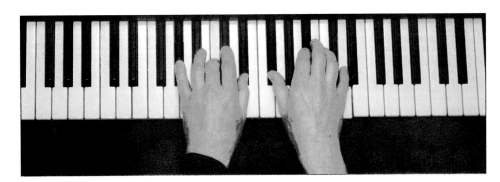

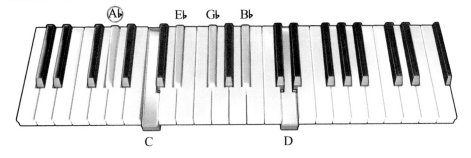

A♭13

A♭

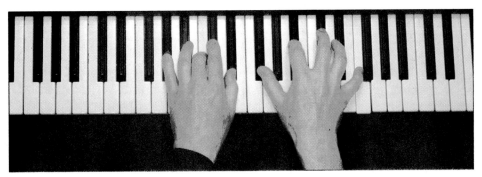

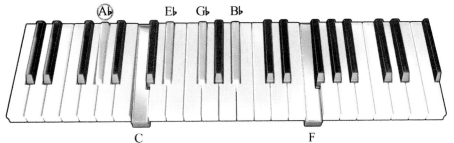

Ab13sus4

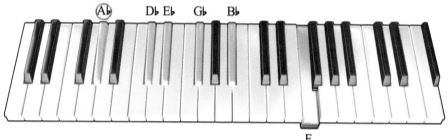

Ab13b5

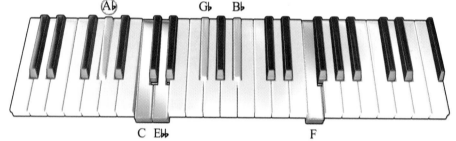

Ab13#5

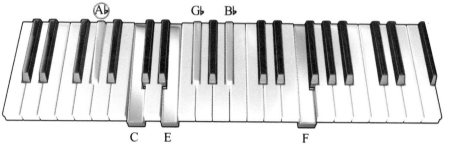

Ab13b9

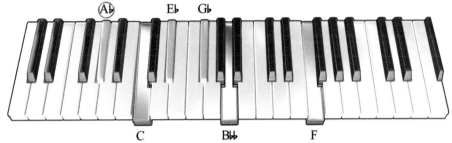

Ab13#9

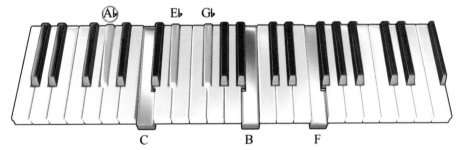

Ab13b5b9

Ab

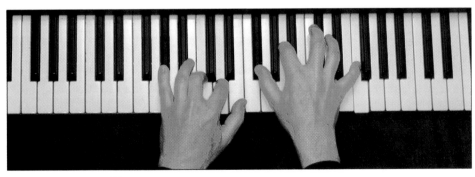

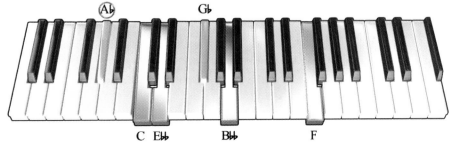

Ab13b5#9

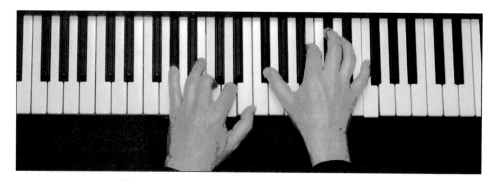

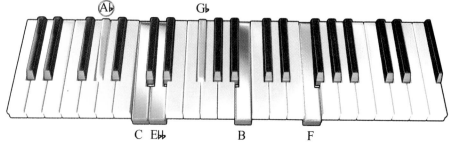

Ab13#5b9

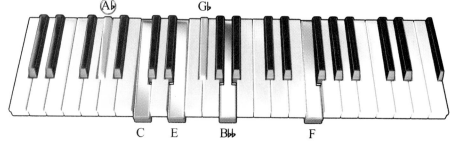

Ab13#5#9

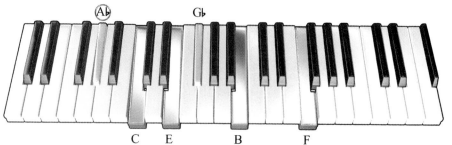

A♭ 6/9

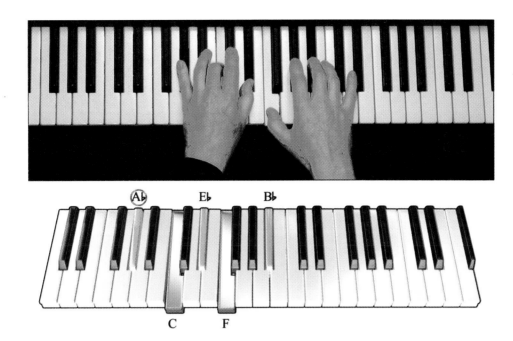

A♭   E♭   B♭

C   F

A♭ major9

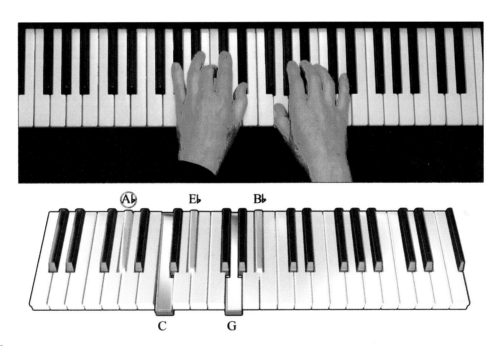

A♭   E♭   B♭

C   G

A♭ major9#11

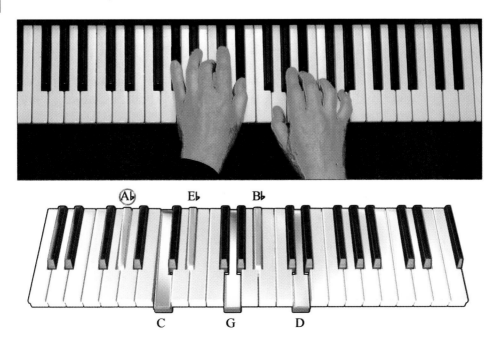

A♭   E♭   B♭

C   G   D

A♭

Ab major13

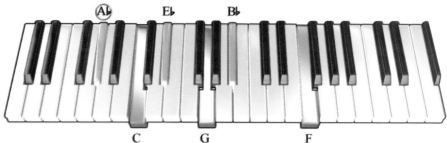

Ab major13b5

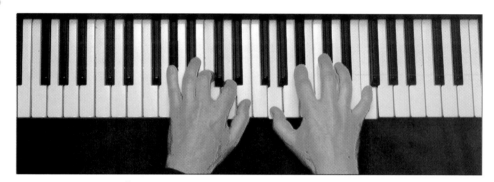

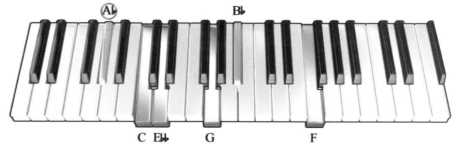

Ab major13#5

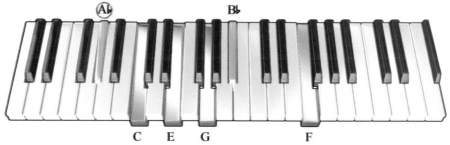

A♭ major13♭9

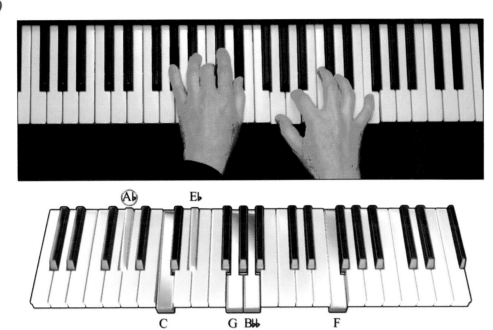

A♭   E♭

C   G B♭♭   F

A♭ major13♯9

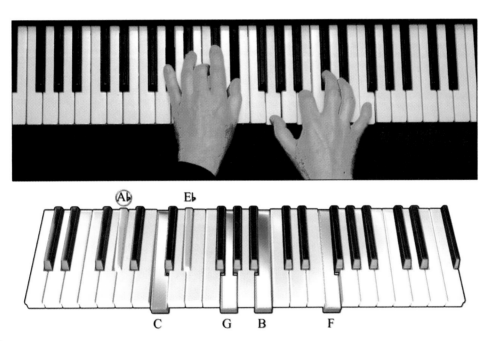

A♭   E♭

C   G   B   F

A♭ major13♭5♭9

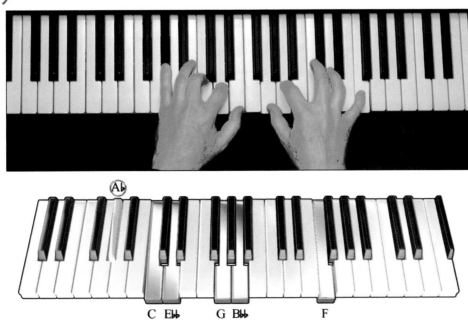

A♭

C E♭♭   G B♭♭   F

A♭

Ab major13b5#9

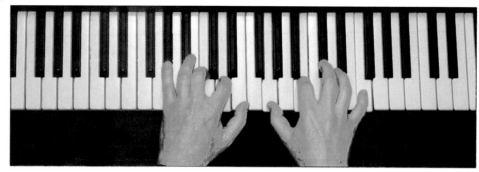

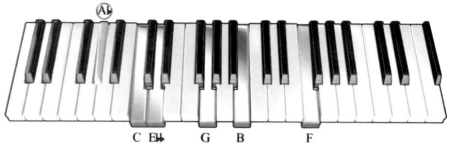

C Ebb   G   B   F

Ab major13#5b9

C   E   G Bbb   F

Ab major13#5#9

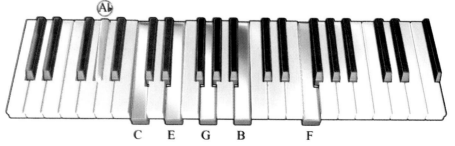

C   E   G   B   F

A♭ minor7♭9

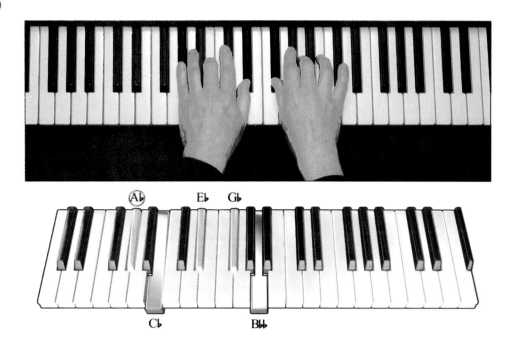

A♭ minor9

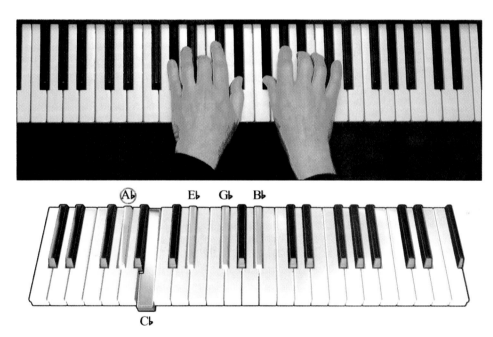

A♭ minor11

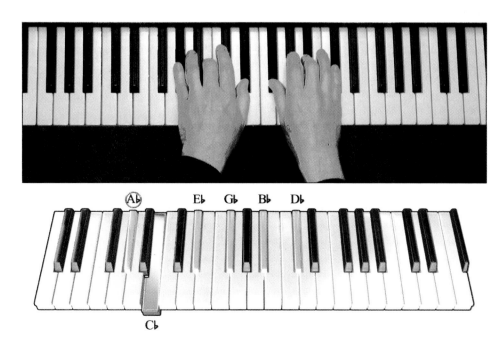

A♭

A♭ minor13

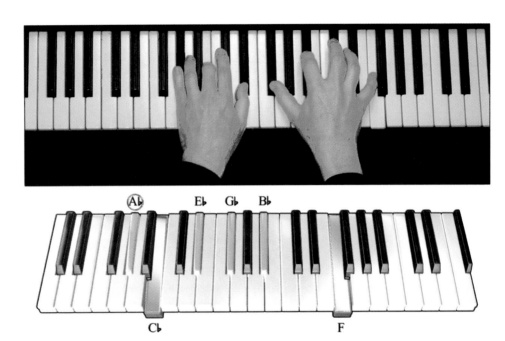

A♭ minor9 (major7)

A chords

A major

A/C# *(first inversion)*

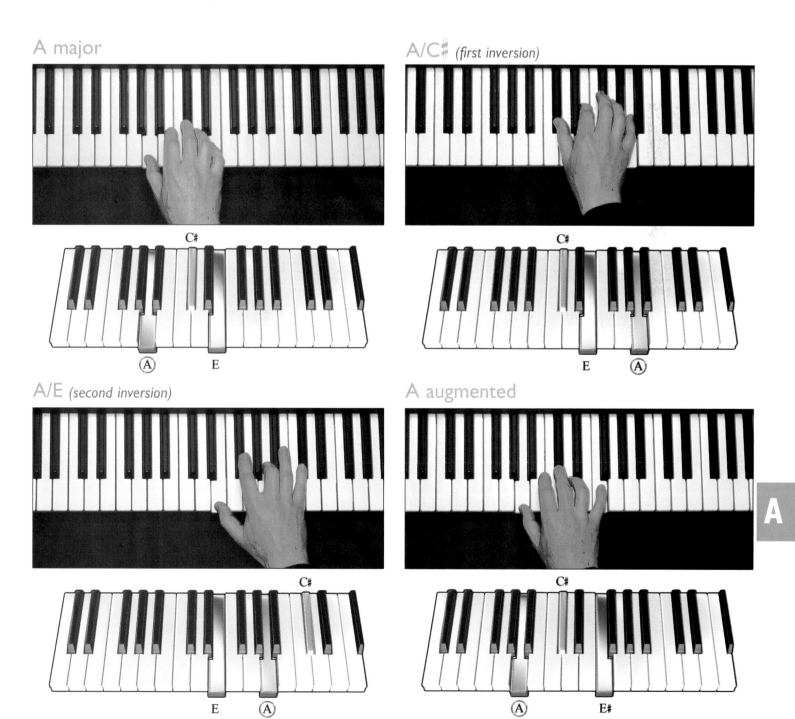

A/E *(second inversion)*

A augmented

A augmented *(first inversion)*

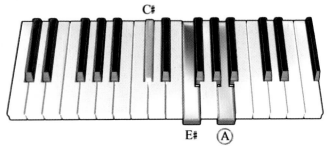

C#

E#   Ⓐ

A augmented *(second inversion)*

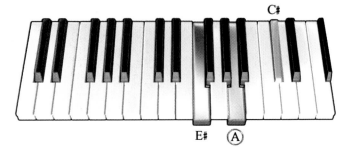

C#

E#   Ⓐ

Asus4

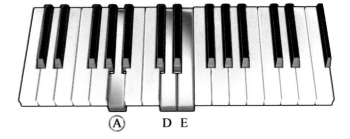

Ⓐ   D E

Asus4 *(first inversion)*

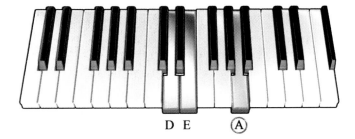

D E   Ⓐ

Asus4 *(second inversion)*

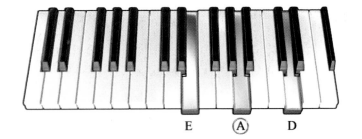

E   Ⓐ   D

A6

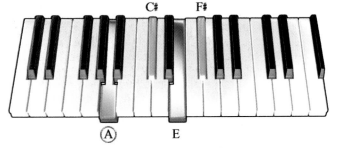

C#   F#

Ⓐ   E

A6 *(first inversion)*

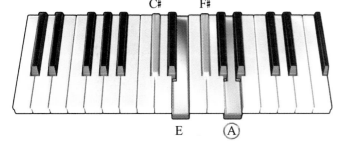

C#   F#

E   (A)

A6 *(second inversion)*

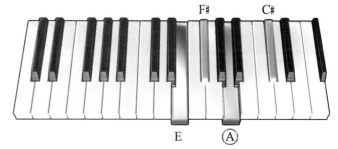

F#   C#

E   (A)

A6 *(third inversion)*

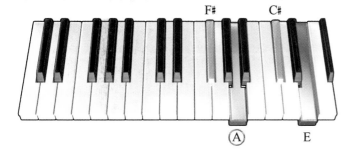

F#   C#

(A)   E

A7

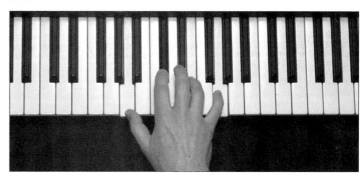

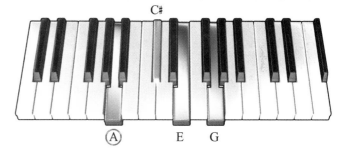

C#

(A)   E   G

A7 *(first inversion)*

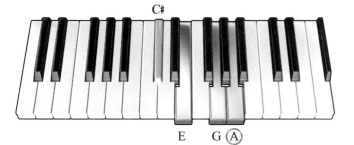

C#

E   G (A)

A7 *(second inversion)*

C#

E   G (A)

A

A7 (third inversion)

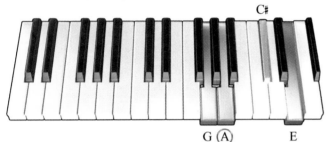

C#

G (A)   E

A°7

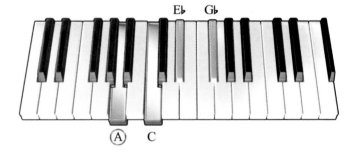

Eb   Gb

(A)   C

A°7 (first inversion)

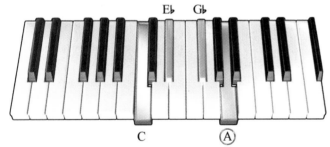

Eb   Gb

C   (A)

A°7 (second inversion)

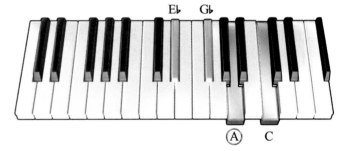

Eb   Gb

(A)   C

A°7 (third inversion)

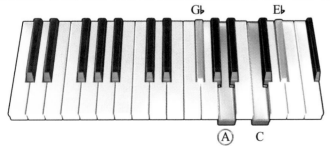

Gb   Eb

(A)   C

A major7

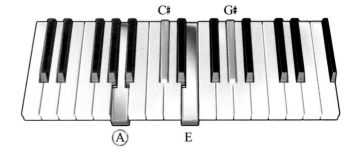

C#   G#

(A)   E

A major7 (first inversion)

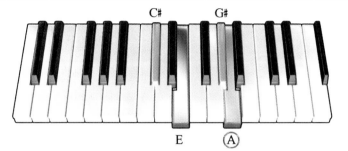

C# G#

E Ⓐ

A major7 (second inversion)

G# C#

E Ⓐ

A major7 (third inversion)

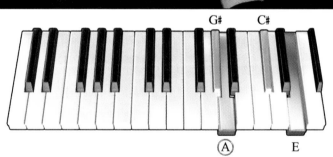

G# C#

Ⓐ E

A minor

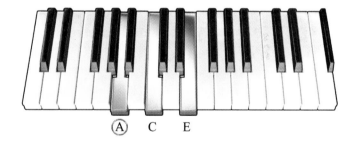

Ⓐ C E

A minor (first inversion)

C E Ⓐ

A minor (second inversion)

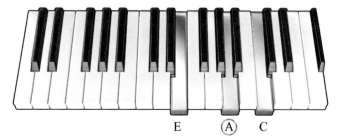

E Ⓐ C

A

A minor6

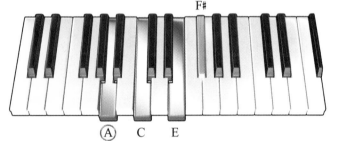

Ⓐ   C   E

A minor6 *(first inversion)*

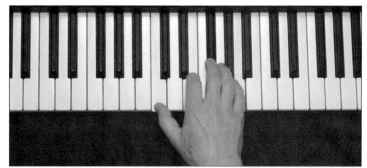

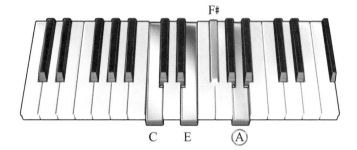

C   E   Ⓐ

A minor6 *(second inversion)*

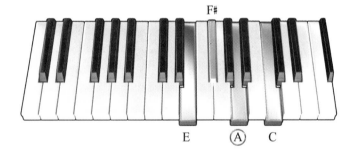

E   Ⓐ   C

A minor6 *(third inversion)*

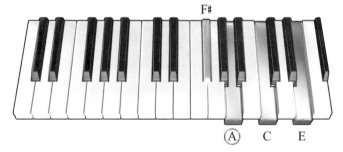

Ⓐ   C   E

A minor7

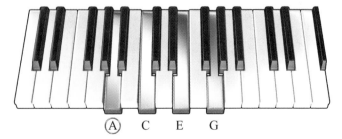

Ⓐ   C   E   G

A minor7 *(first inversion)*

C   E   GⒶ

A minor7 (second inversion)

E   G (A)   C

A minor7 (third inversion)

G (A)   C   E

A minor7♭5

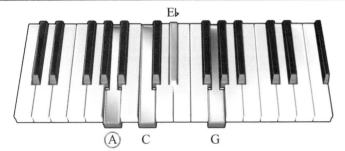

E♭

(A)   C   G

A minor7♭5 (first inversion)

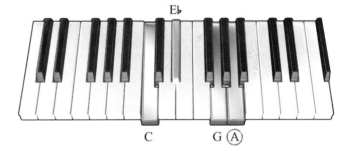

E♭

C   G (A)

A minor7♭5 (second inversion)

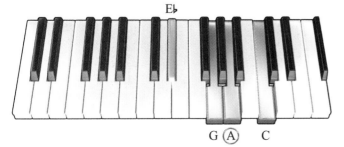

E♭

G (A)   C

A minor7♭5 (third inversion)

E♭

G (A)   C

A

A minor (major7)

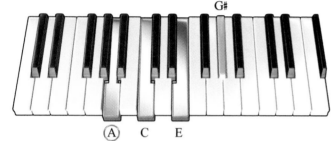

G#

Ⓐ C E

A minor (major7) *(first inversion)*

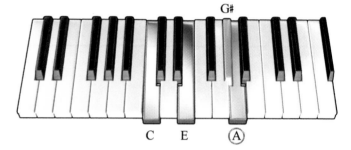

G#

C E Ⓐ

A minor (major7) *(second inversion)*

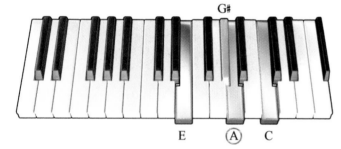

G#

E Ⓐ C

A minor (major7) *(third inversion)*

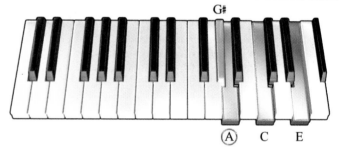

G#

Ⓐ C E

A chords
using both hands

A7♭9

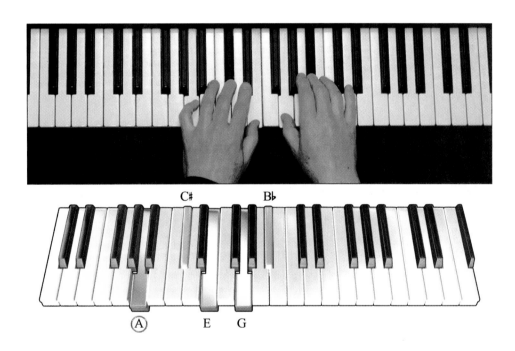

C#   B♭

Ⓐ   E   G

A7#9

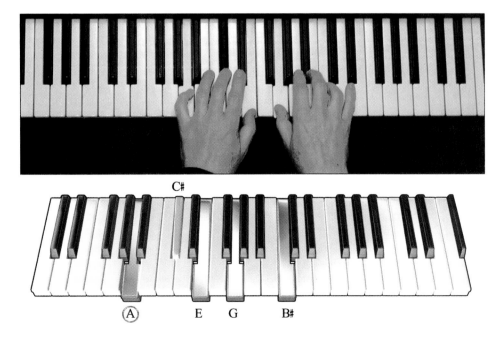

C#

Ⓐ   E   G   B#

A

A9

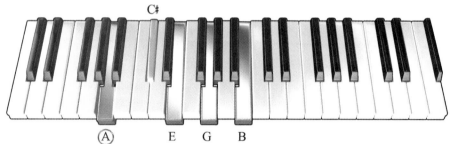

A9sus4

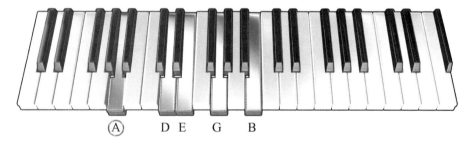

A9♭5

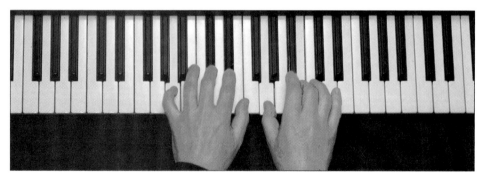

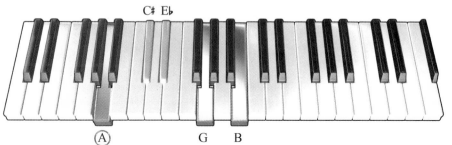

A9#5

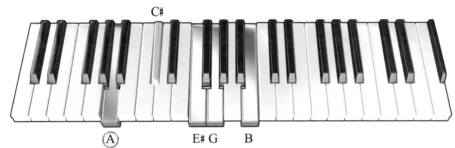

C#

Ⓐ   E# G   B

A9#11

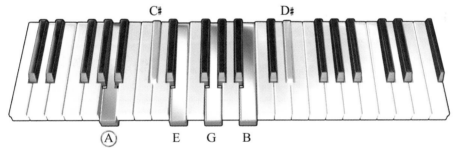

C#   D#

Ⓐ   E   G   B

A13

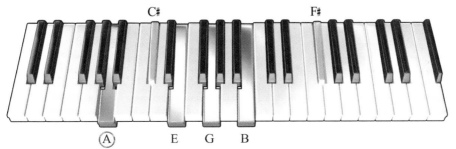

C#   F#

Ⓐ   E   G   B

A

A13sus4

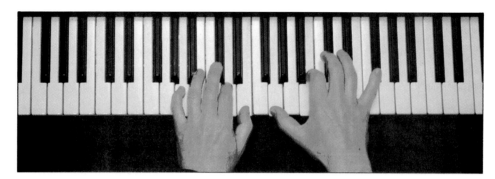

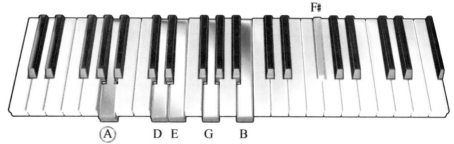

Ⓐ D E G B F#

A13♭5

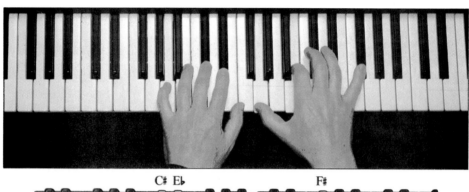

C# E♭ F#

Ⓐ G B

A13#5

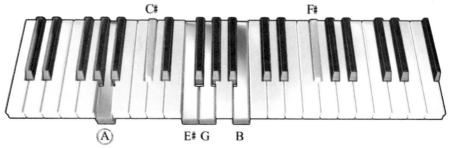

C# F#

Ⓐ E# G B

A13♭9

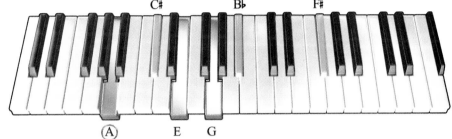

C♯   B♭   F♯

Ⓐ   E   G

A13♯9

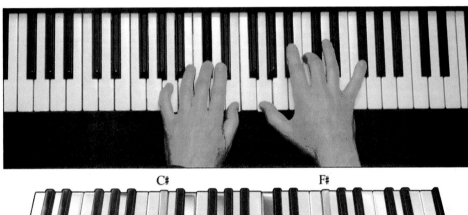

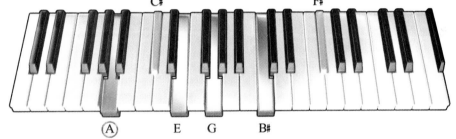

C♯   F♯

Ⓐ   E   G   B♯

A13♭5♭9

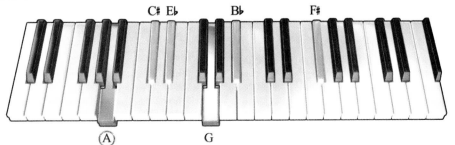

C♯ E♭   B♭   F♯

Ⓐ   G

A

A13♭5♯9

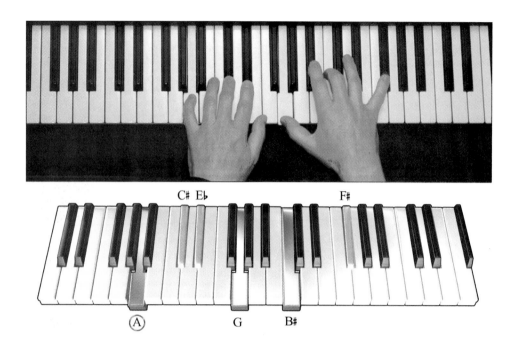

C♯ E♭   F♯

Ⓐ   G   B♯

A13♯5♭9

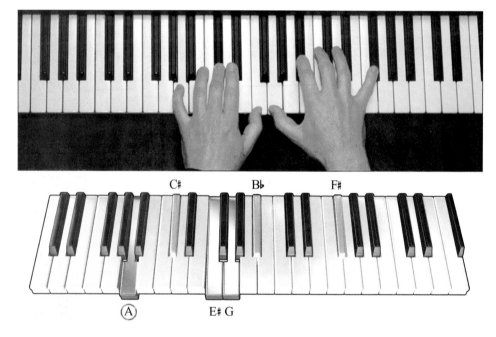

C♯   B♭   F♯

Ⓐ   E♯ G

A13♯5♯9

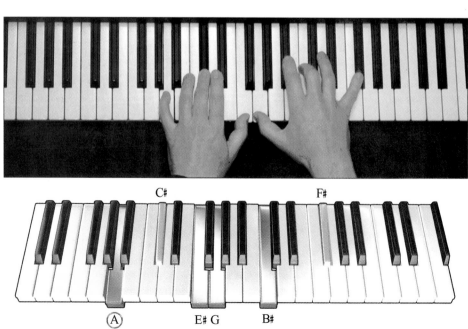

C♯   F♯

Ⓐ   E♯ G   B♯

A 6/9

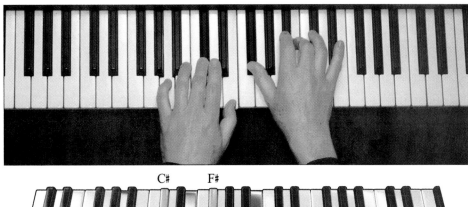

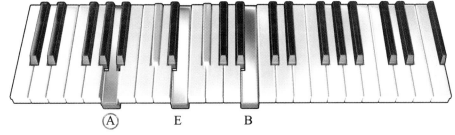

A major9

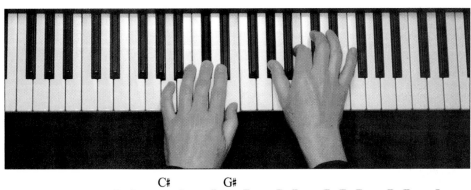

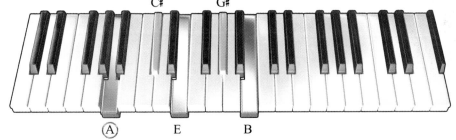

A major9#11

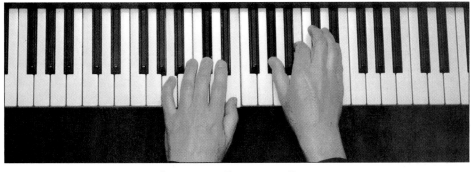

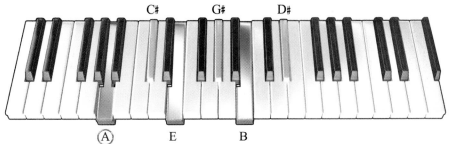

A

A major13

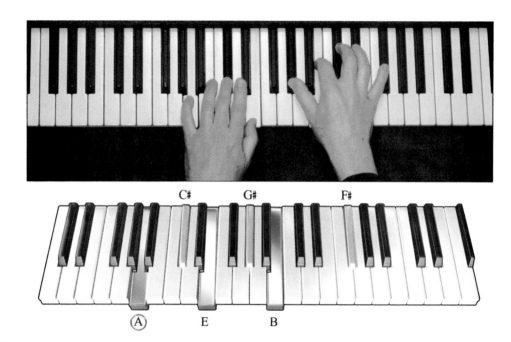

A major13♭5

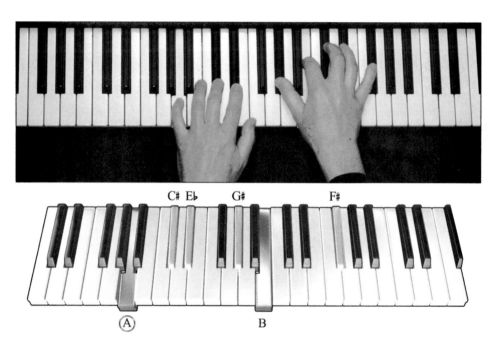

A major13♯5

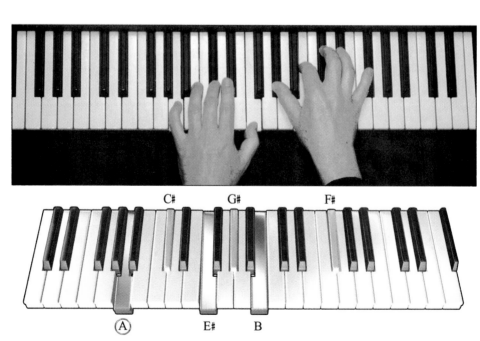

A major13♭9

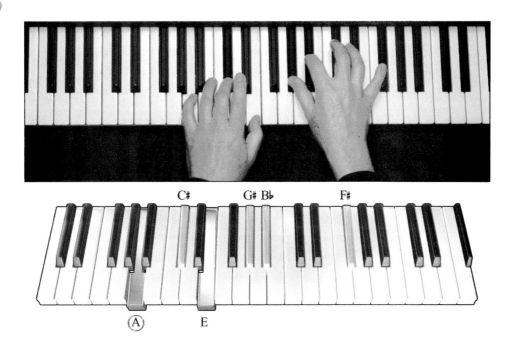

A major13♯9

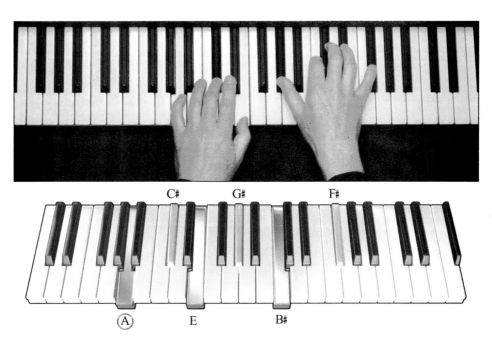

A major13♭5♭9

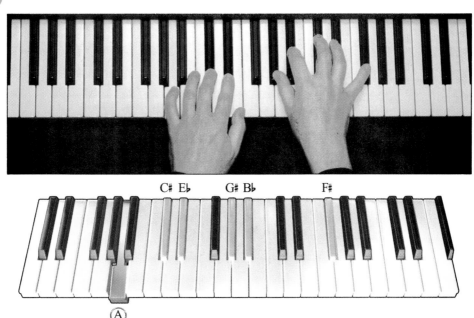

A

A major13♭5♯9

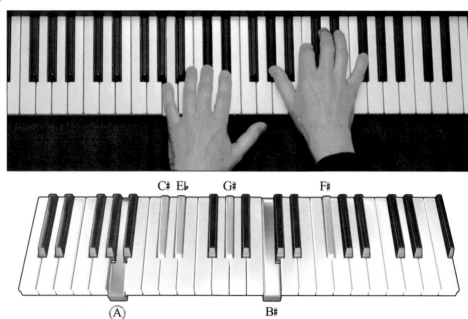

A major13♯5♭9

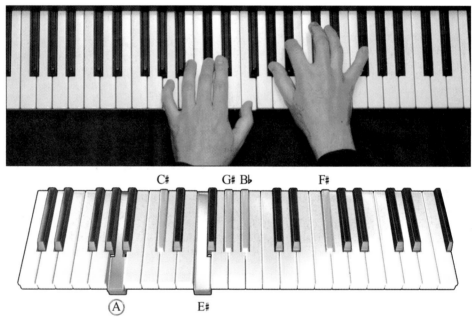

A major13♯5♯9

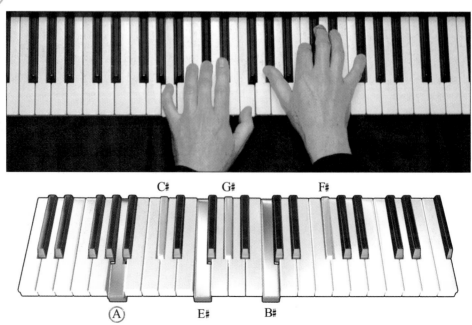

A minor7♭9

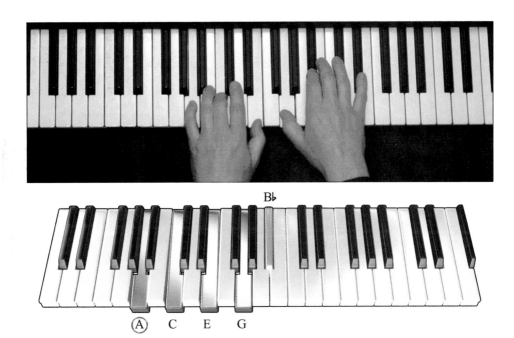

B♭

Ⓐ   C   E   G

A minor9

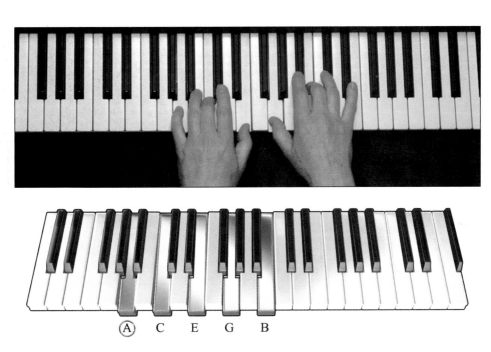

Ⓐ   C   E   G   B

A minor11

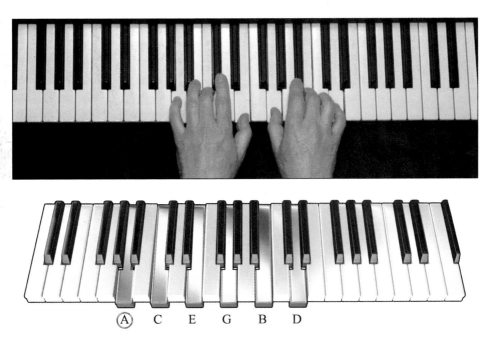

Ⓐ   C   E   G   B   D

A

A minor13

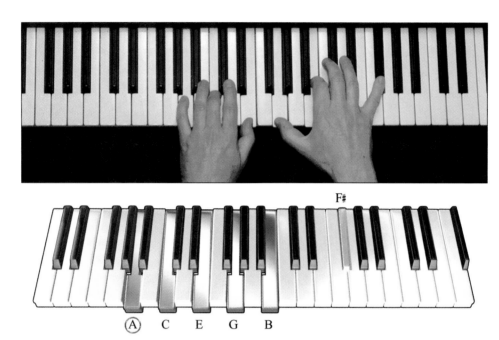

F#

(A) C   E   G   B

A minor9 (major7)

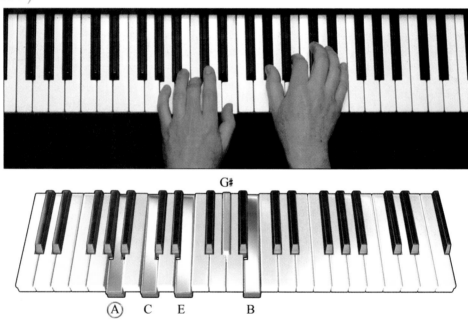

G#

(A) C   E   B

B♭ chords

B♭ major

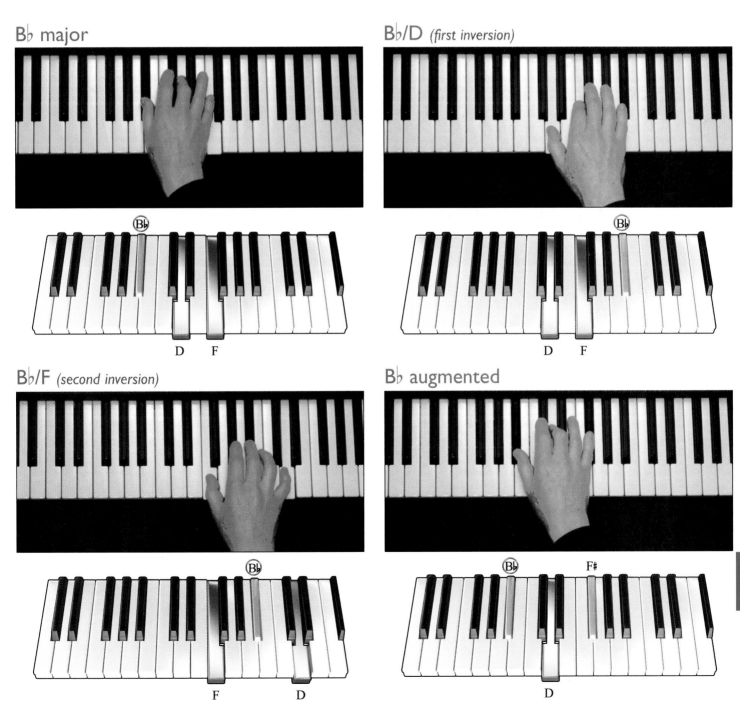

B♭/D *(first inversion)*

B♭/F *(second inversion)*

B♭ augmented

B♭

B♭ augmented *(first inversion)*

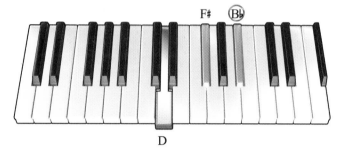

F# B♭

D

B♭ augmented *(second inversion)*

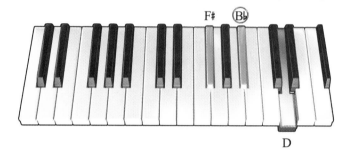

F# B♭

D

B♭sus4

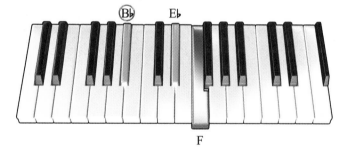

B♭ E♭

F

B♭sus4 *(first inversion)*

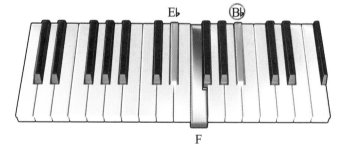

E♭ B♭

F

B♭sus4 *(second inversion)*

B♭ E♭

F

B♭6

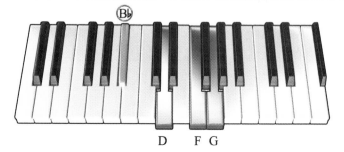

B♭

D F G

B♭6 *(first inversion)*

D   F G

B♭6 *(second inversion)*

F G   D

B♭6 *(third inversion)*

G   D   F

B♭7

D   F

B♭7 *(first inversion)*

D   F

B♭7 *(second inversion)*

F   D

B♭

B♭7 (third inversion)

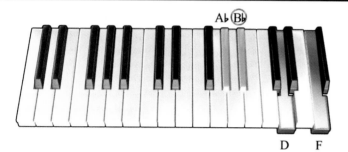

A♭ (B♭)

D   F

B♭°7

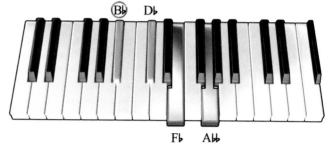

(B♭)   D♭

F♭   A♭♭

B♭°7 (first inversion)

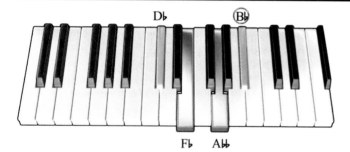

D♭   (B♭)

F♭   A♭♭

B♭°7 (second inversion)

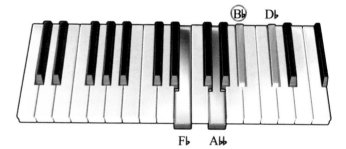

(B♭)   D♭

F♭   A♭♭

B♭°7 (third inversion)

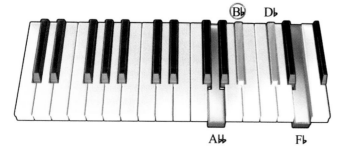

(B♭) D♭

A♭♭   F♭

B♭ major7

(B♭)

D   F   A

B♭ major7 *(first inversion)*

B♭ D F A

B♭ major7 *(second inversion)*

B♭ F A D

B♭ major7 *(third inversion)*

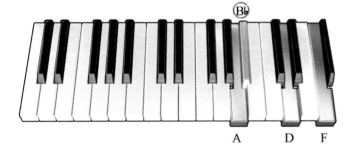

B♭ A D F

B♭ minor

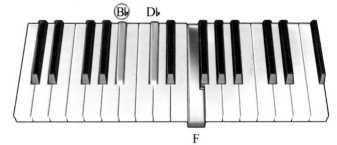

B♭ D♭ F

B♭ minor *(first inversion)*

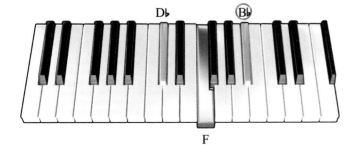

D♭ B♭ F

B♭ minor *(second inversion)*

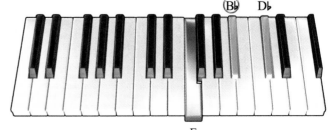

B♭ D♭ F

B♭

B♭ minor6

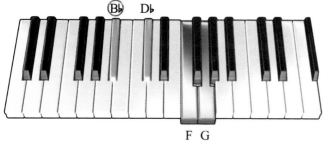

B♭ minor6 *(first inversion)*

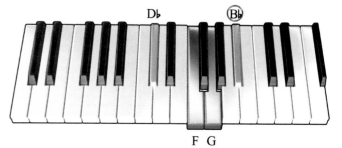

B♭ minor6 *(second inversion)*

B♭ minor6 *(third inversion)*

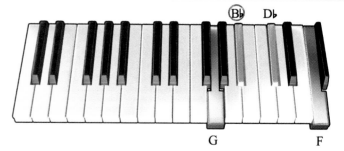

B♭ minor7

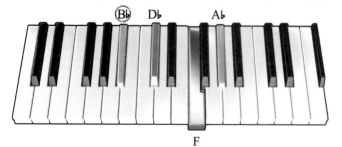

B♭ minor7 *(first inversion)*

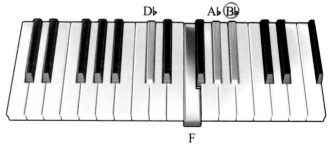

B♭ minor7 *(second inversion)*

A♭ (B♭) D♭

F

B♭ minor7♭5

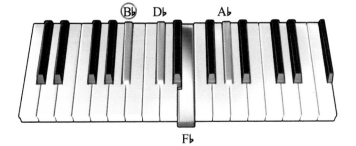

(B♭) D♭ A♭

F♭

B♭ minor7♭5 *(second inversion)*

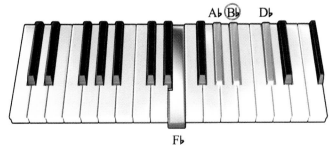

A♭ (B♭) D♭

F♭

B♭ minor7 *(third inversion)*

A♭ (B♭) D♭

F

B♭ minor7♭5 *(first inversion)*

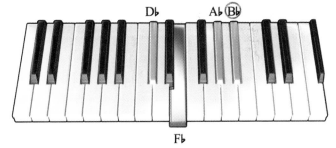

D♭ A♭ (B♭)

F♭

B♭ minor7♭5 *(third inversion)*

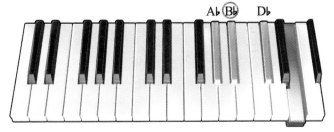

A♭ (B♭) D♭

F♭

B♭

B♭ minor (major7)

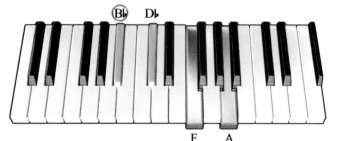

B♭ minor (major7) *(first inversion)*

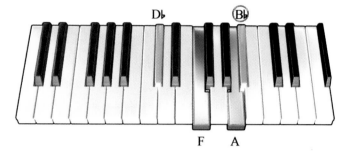

B♭ minor (major7) *(second inversion)*

B♭ minor (major7) *(third inversion)*

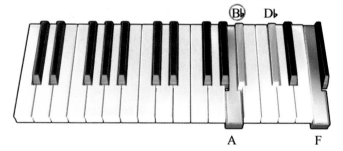

B♭ chords
using both hands

B♭7♭9

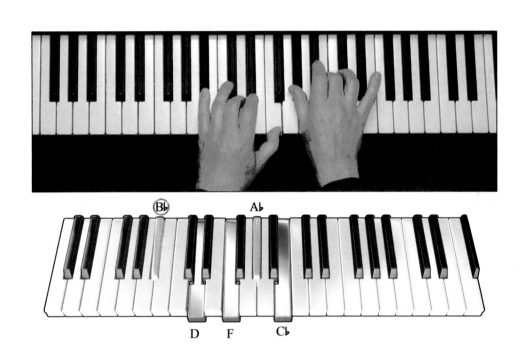

B♭7♯9

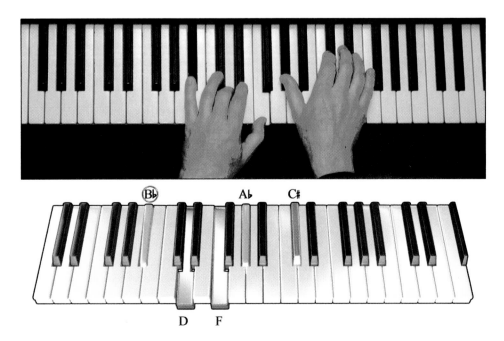

B♭

B♭9

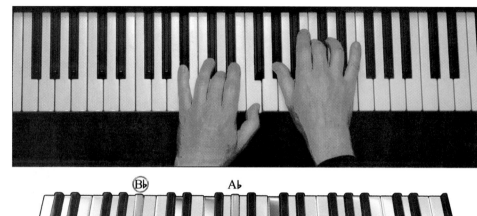

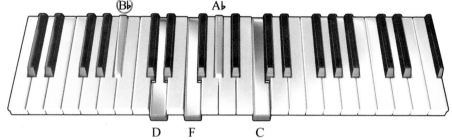

D   F   C

B♭9sus4

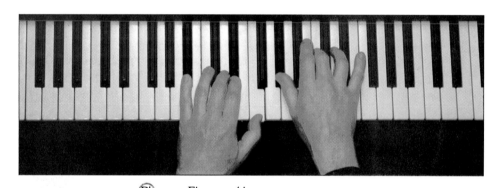

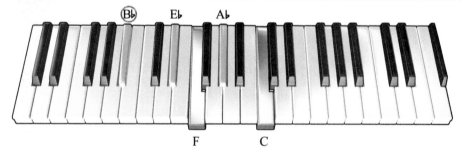

F   C

B♭9♭5

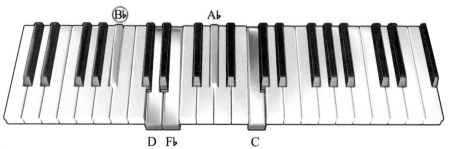

D F♭   C

B♭9♯5

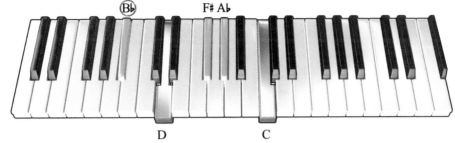

B♭   F♯ A♭

D   C

B♭9♯11

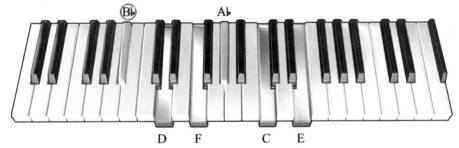

B♭   A♭

D   F   C   E

B♭13

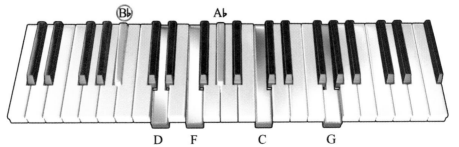

B♭   A♭

D   F   C   G

B♭

Bb13sus4

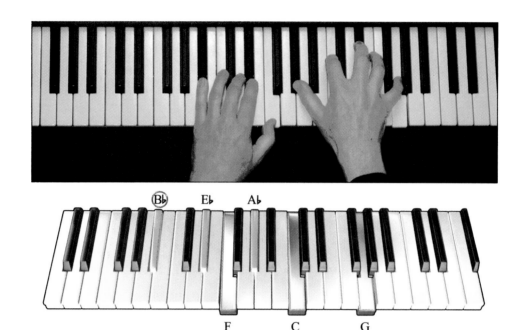

Bb   Eb   Ab

F   C   G

Bb13b5

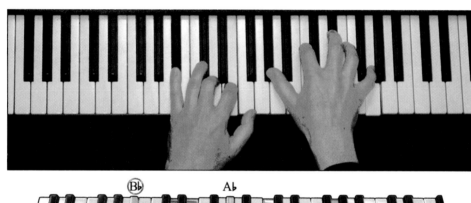

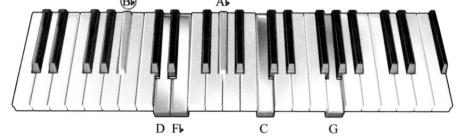

Bb   Ab

D Fb   C   G

Bb13#5

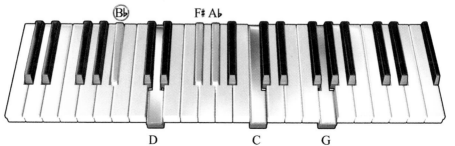

Bb   F# Ab

D   C   G

B♭13♭9

B♭   A♭

D   F   C♭   G

B♭13♯9

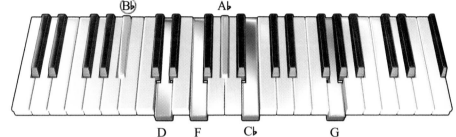

B♭   A♭   C♯

D   F   G

B♭13♭5♭9

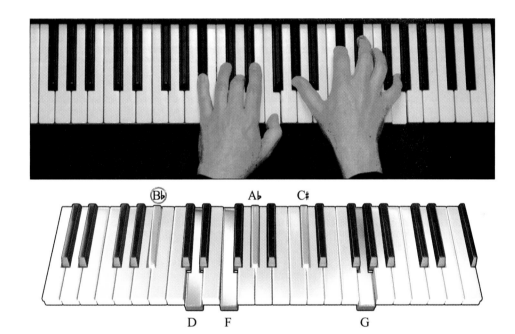

B♭   A♭

D F♭   C♭   G

B♭

B♭13♭5♯9

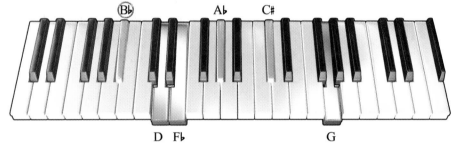

B♭13♯5♭9

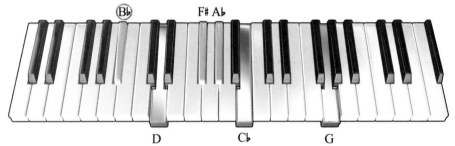

B♭13♯5♯9

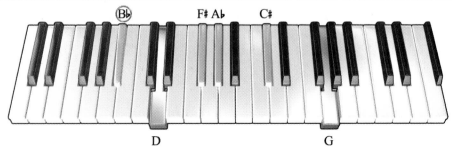

B♭ 6/9

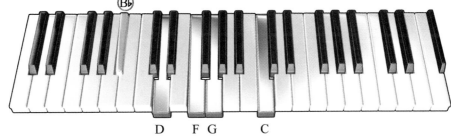

D   F G   C

B♭ major9

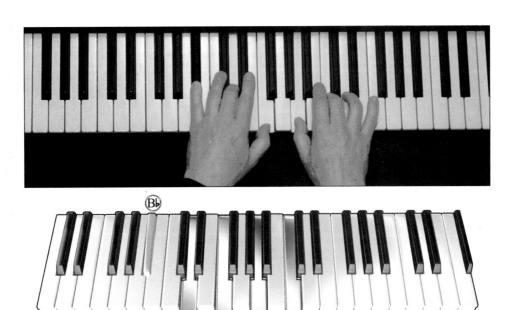

D   F   A   C

B♭ major9♯11

D   F   A   C   E

B♭

B♭ major13

D   F   A   C   G

B♭ major13♭5

D   F♭   A   C   G

B♭ major13♯5

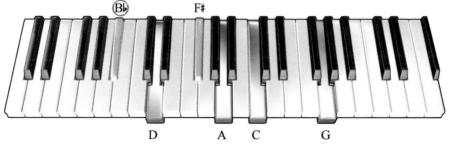

D   A   C   G

B♭ major13♭9

B♭   D   F   A C♭   G

B♭ major13♯9

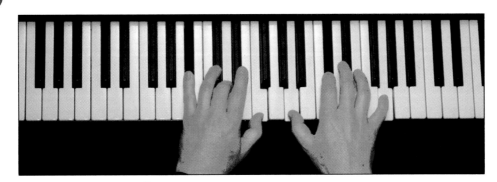

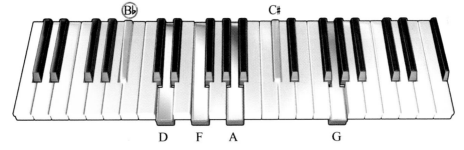

B♭   C♯   D   F   A   G

B♭ major13♭5♭9

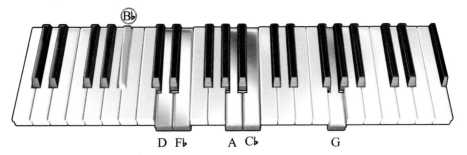

B♭   D F♭   A C♭   G

B♭

B♭ major13♭5♯9

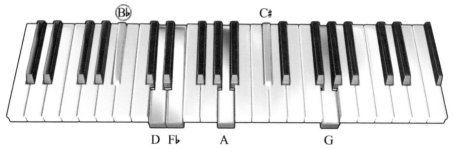

B♭ major13♯5♭9

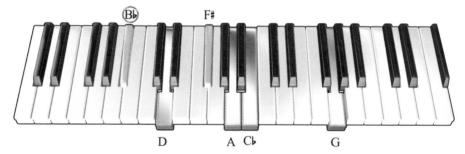

B♭ major13♯5♯9

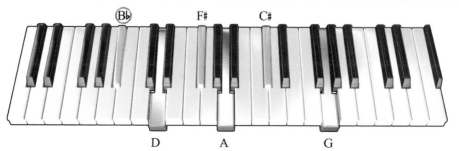

B♭ minor7♭9

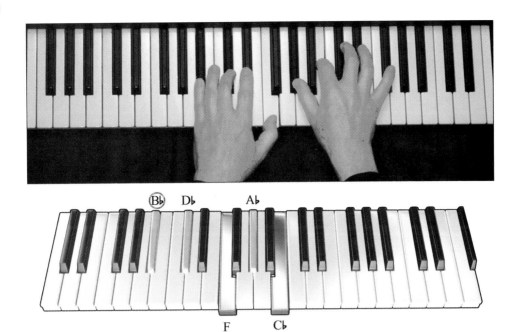

B♭ minor9

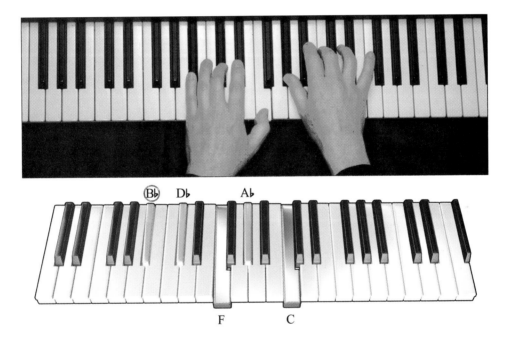

B♭ minor11

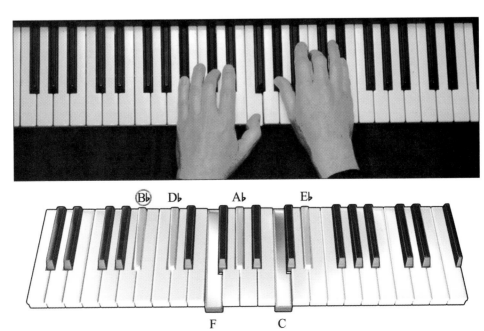

B♭

Bb minor13

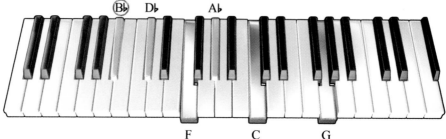

Bb minor9 (major7)

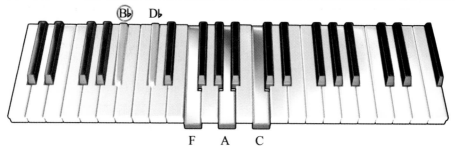

B chords

B major

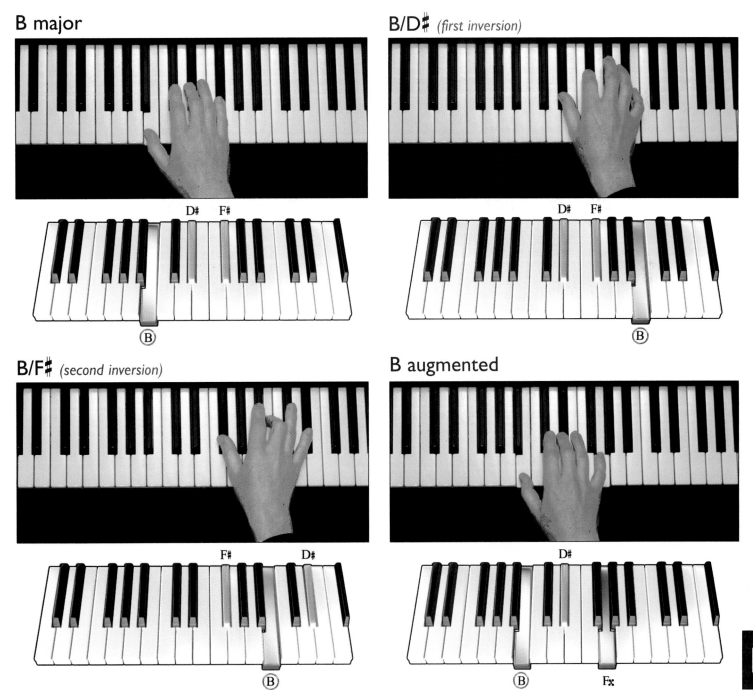

B/D♯ *(first inversion)*

B/F♯ *(second inversion)*

B augmented

B

B augmented *(first inversion)*

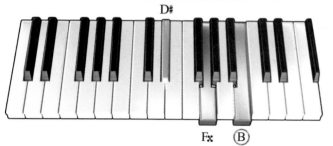

D#

Fx Ⓑ

B augmented *(second inversion)*

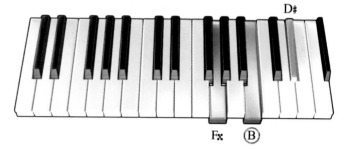

D#

Fx Ⓑ

Bsus4

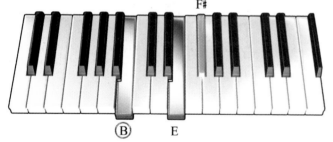

F#

Ⓑ E

Bsus4 *(first inversion)*

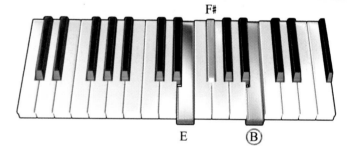

F#

E Ⓑ

Bsus4 *(second inversion)*

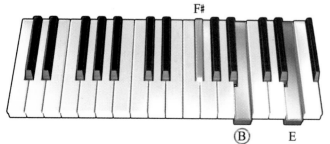

F#

Ⓑ E

B6

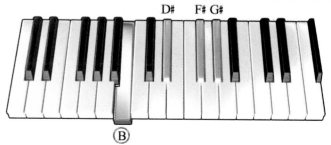

D# F# G#

Ⓑ

B6 (first inversion)

D# F# G#

B

B6 (second inversion)

F# G# D#

B

B6 (third inversion)

G# D# F#

B

B7

D# F#

B A

B7 (first inversion)

D# F#

A B

B7 (second inversion)

F# D#

A B

B

B7 (third inversion)

D#   F#

A (B)

B°7

A♭

(B)   D   F

B°7 (first inversion)

A♭

D   F   (B)

B°7 (second inversion)

A♭

F   (B)   D

B°7 (third inversion)

A♭

(B)   D   F

B major7

D#   F#   A#

(B)

B major7 *(first inversion)*

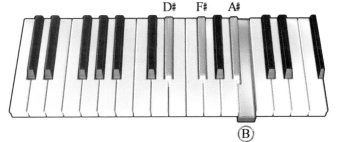

D# F# A#

Ⓑ

B major7 *(second inversion)*

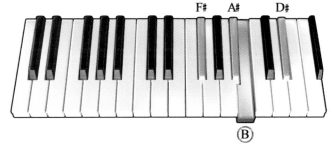

F# A# D#

Ⓑ

B major7 *(third inversion)*

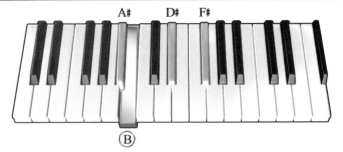

A# D# F#

Ⓑ

B minor

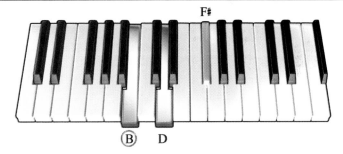

F#

Ⓑ D

B minor *(first inversion)*

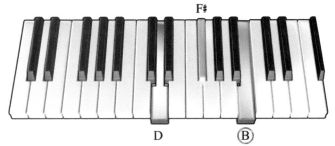

F#

D Ⓑ

B minor *(second inversion)*

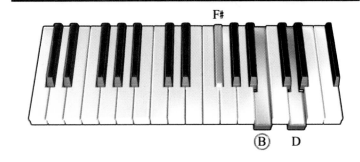

F#

Ⓑ D

B

B minor6

F# G#

Ⓑ D

B minor6 *(first inversion)*

F# G#

D Ⓑ

B minor6 *(second inversion)*

F# G#

Ⓑ D

B minor6 *(third inversion)*

G# F#

Ⓑ D

B minor7

F#

Ⓑ D A

B minor7 *(first inversion)*

F#

D A Ⓑ

B minor7 *(second inversion)*

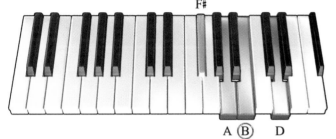

F#

A Ⓑ   D

B minor7 *(third inversion)*

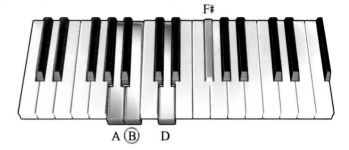

F#

A Ⓑ   D

B minor7♭5

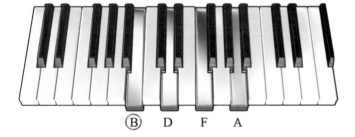

Ⓑ   D   F   A

B minor7♭5 *(first inversion)*

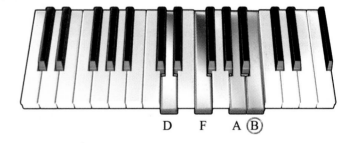

D   F   A Ⓑ

B minor7♭5 *(second inversion)*

F   A Ⓑ   D

B minor7♭5 *(third inversion)*

A Ⓑ   D   F

B

B minor (major7)

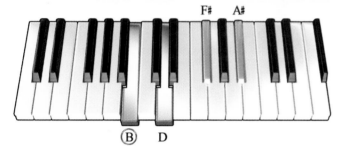

B minor (major7) *(first inversion)*

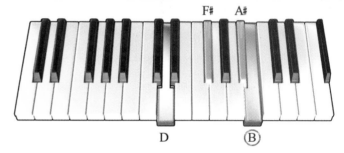

B minor (major7) *(second inversion)*

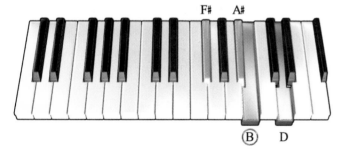

B minor (major7) *(third inversion)*

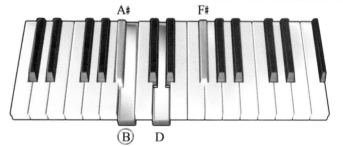

B chords
using both hands

B7♭9

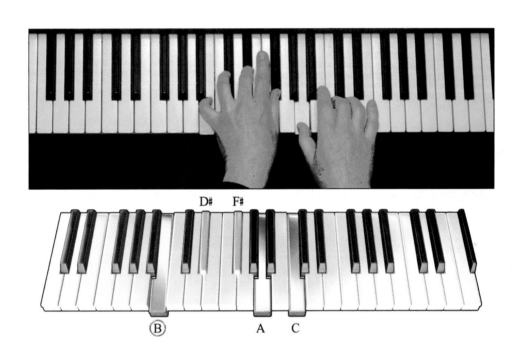

D#   F#

Ⓑ   A   C

B7♯9

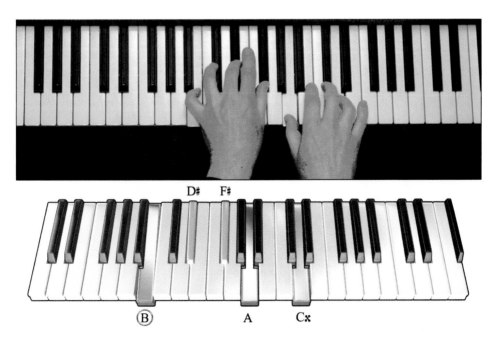

D#   F#

Ⓑ   A   C𝄪

B

239

B9

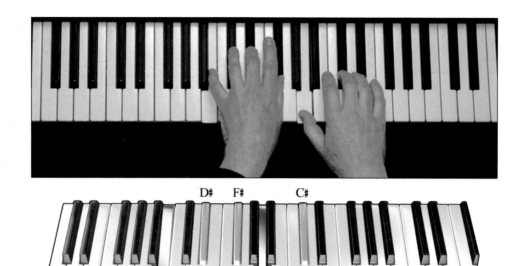

B9sus4

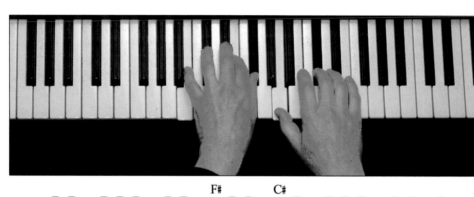

B9♭5

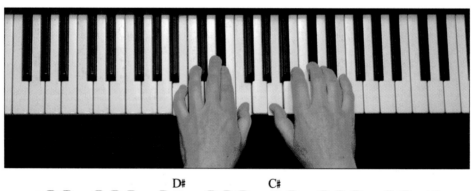

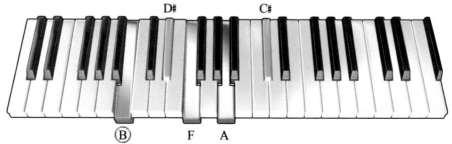

B9#5

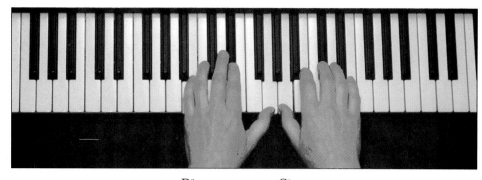

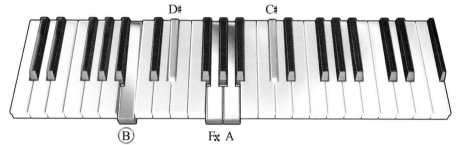

B9#11

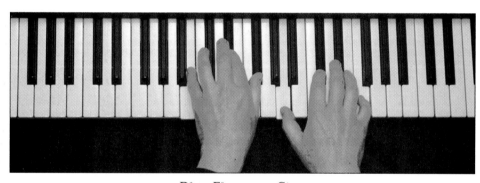

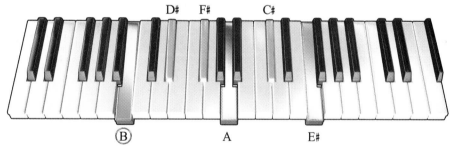

B13

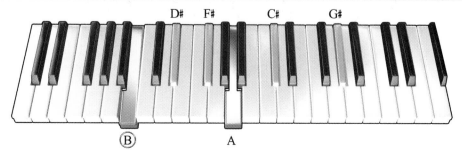

B

B13sus4

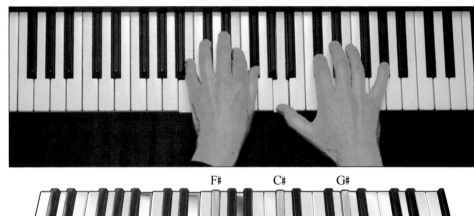

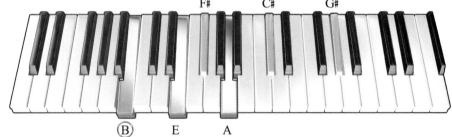

B13♭5

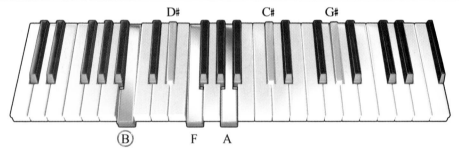

B13♯5

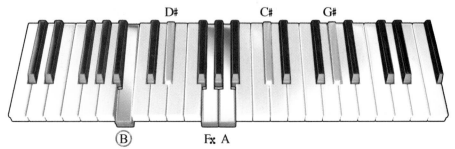

B13♭9

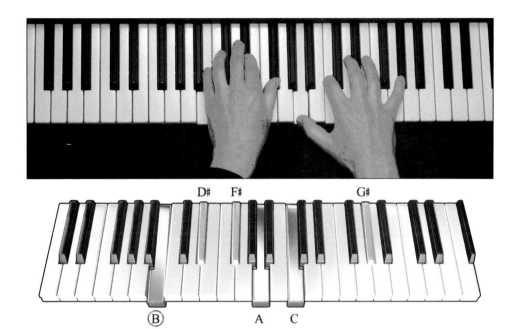

B13♯9

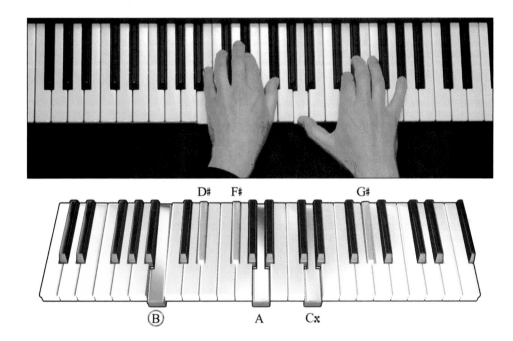

B13♭5♭9

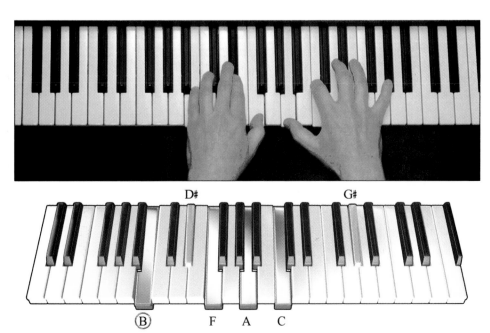

B

B13♭5♯9

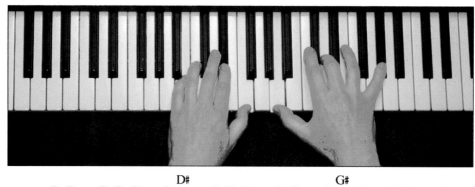

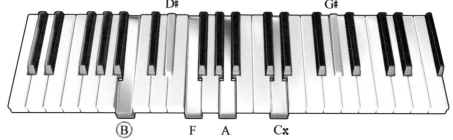

D#   G#

Ⓑ   F   A   C✗

B13♯5♭9

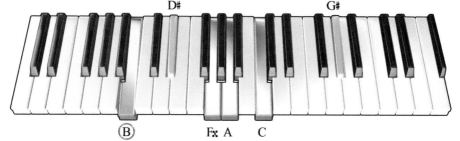

D#   G#

Ⓑ   F✗ A   C

B13♯5♯9

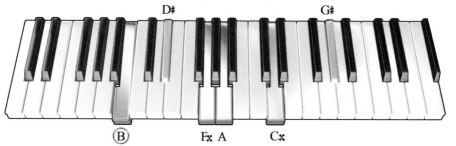

D#   G#

Ⓑ   F✗ A   C✗

B 6/9

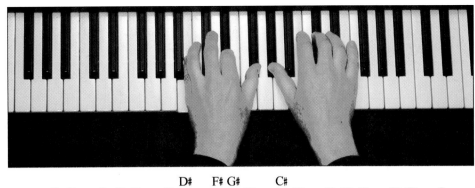

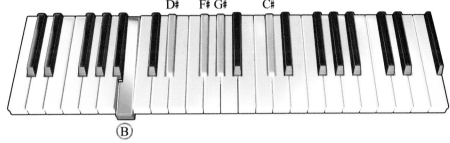

D#   F# G#   C#

Ⓑ

B major9

D#   F#   A#   C#

Ⓑ

B major9#11

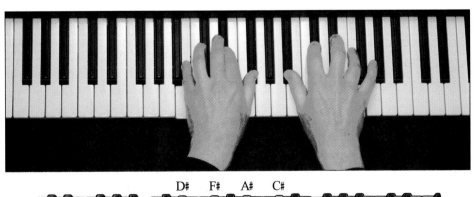

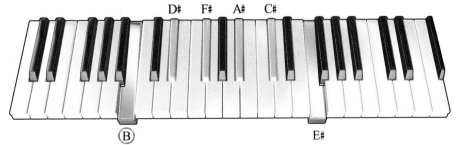

D#   F#   A#   C#

Ⓑ   E#

B

B major13

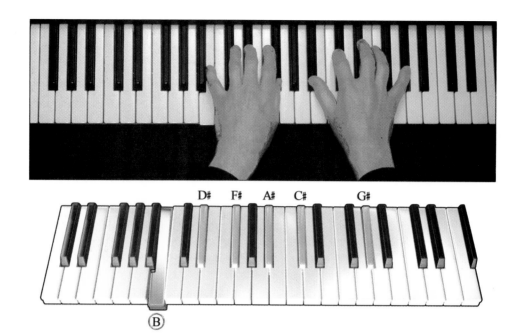

B major13♭5

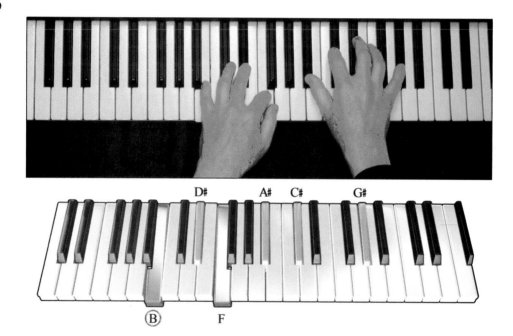

B major13♯5

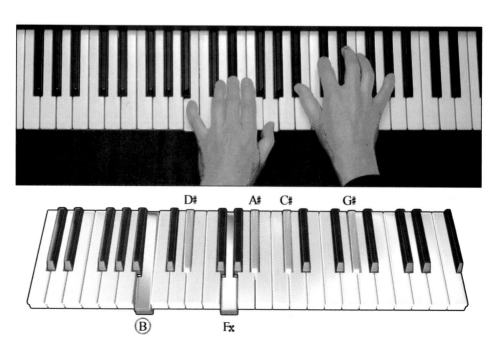

B major13♭9

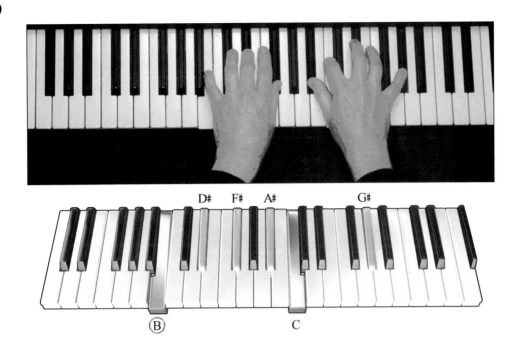

B major13♯9

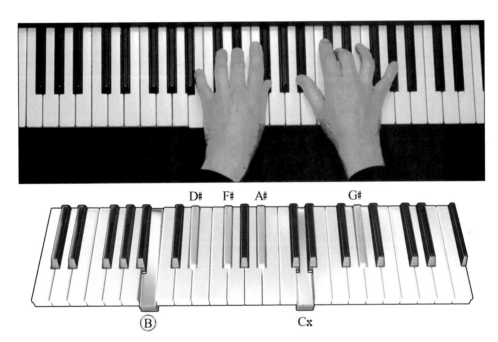

B major13♭5♭9

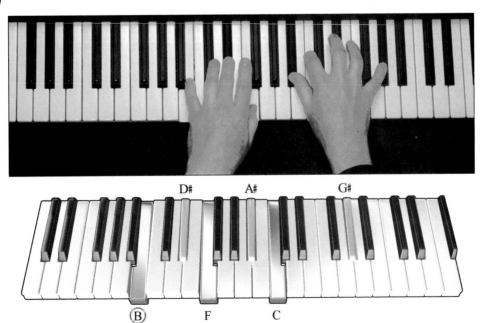

B

B major13♭5♯9

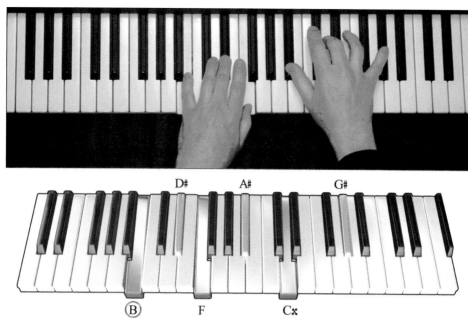

D#   A#   G#

Ⓑ   F   Cx

B major13♯5♭9

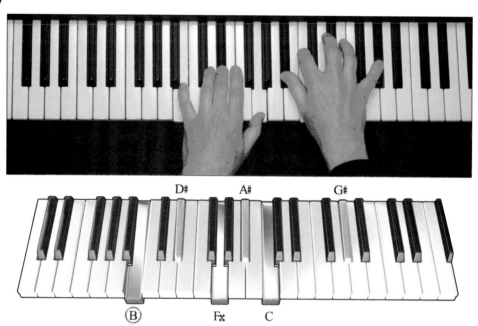

D#   A#   G#

Ⓑ   Fx   C

B major13♯5♯9

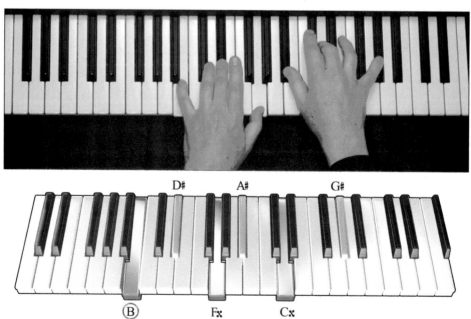

D#   A#   G#

Ⓑ   Fx   Cx

B minor7♭9

F#

Ⓑ D   A   C

B minor9

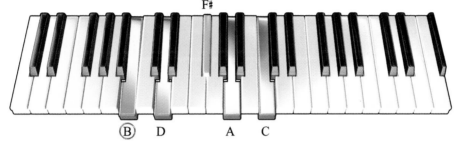

F#   C#

Ⓑ D   A

B minor11

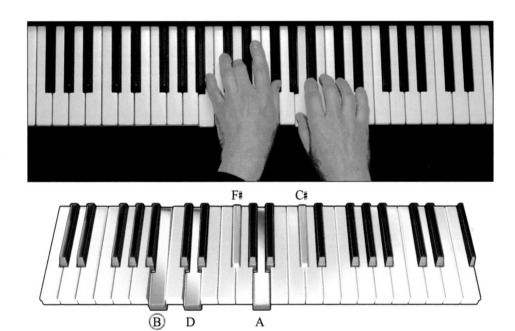

F#   C#

Ⓑ D   A   E

B

B minor13

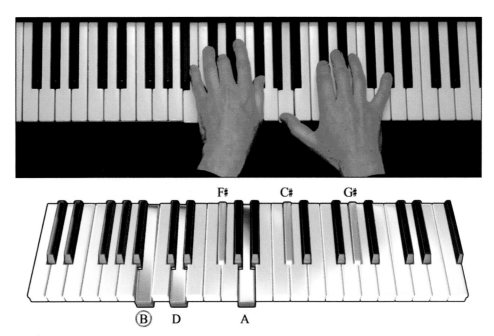

F#   C#   G#

Ⓑ   D   A

B minor9 (major7)

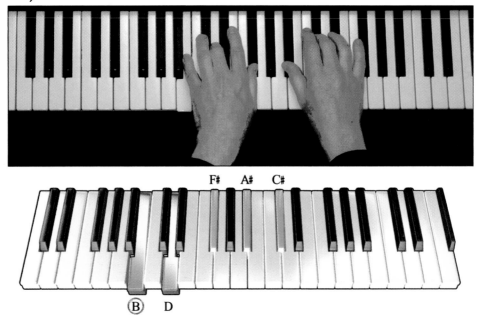

F#   A#   C#

Ⓑ   D

Chord Construction

Scales

In order to talk about chord structure we need to discuss the foundation by which chords are formed—*scales*. There are a multitude of scales available to the musician, but we will explain only those that are most pertinent—the major, minor, and chromatic scales.

Chromatic

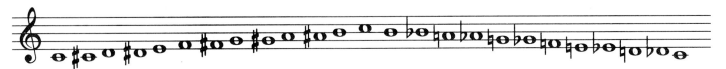

Major

Harmonic minor

Melodic minor

Scales are determined by the distribution of half-tones and whole-tones. For example, the major scale has half-tones between scale steps three and four, and between seven and eight. The harmonic minor has half-tones between scale steps two and three, five and six, and seven and eight. The melodic minor scale's ascending order finds half-steps at six and five and three and two, and a whole-step is now in the place of eight and seven. It is common to refer to scale steps, or *degrees*, by Roman numerals as in the example above and also by the following names:

I.	Tonic
II.	Supertonic
III.	Mediant
IV.	Subdominant
V.	Dominant
VI.	Submediant
VII.	Leading-tone

Intervals

An *interval* is the distance between two notes. This is the basis for harmony (chords). The naming of intervals, as in the example below, is fairly standard, but you may encounter other terminology in various forms of musical literature.

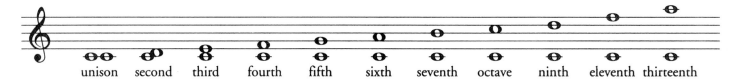

unison second third fourth fifth sixth seventh octave ninth eleventh thirteenth

Chords

Chords are produced by combining two or more intervals, and the simplest of these combinations is a *triad*. A triad consists of three notes obtained by the superposition of two thirds. The notes are called the *root*, the *third*, and the *fifth*.

Inversions

Inversions are produced by arranging the intervals of a chord in a different order. A triad that has the root as the bottom or lowest tone is said to be in *root position*. A triad with a third as the bottom or lowest tone is in *first inversion*, and a triad with a fifth as the bottom or lowest tone is in *second inversion*. As the chords become more complex—such as, sixths, sevenths, etc.—there will be more possible inversions.

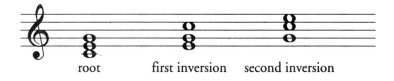

root   first inversion   second inversion

Play *Morning Has Broken* with the suggested inversions. Notice that your fingers are moving one or two keys to the right or left as opposed to moving your whole hand up and down the keyboard. Try playing the same song with the chords in their root position, then go back and play the song with the chord inversions. You will probably notice that the song even sounds better when using inversions, as well as being easier to play. Try using inversions on some of your favorite tunes.

MORNING HAS BROKEN

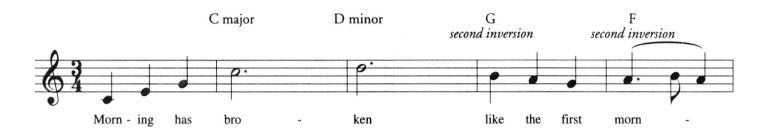

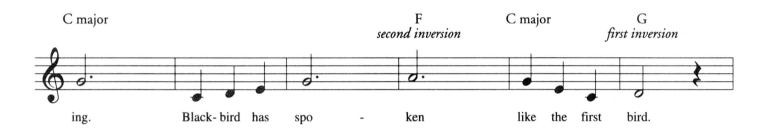

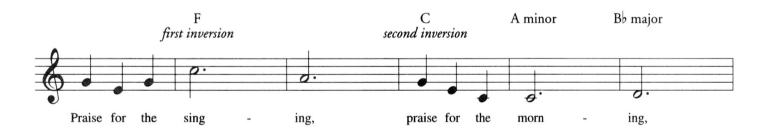

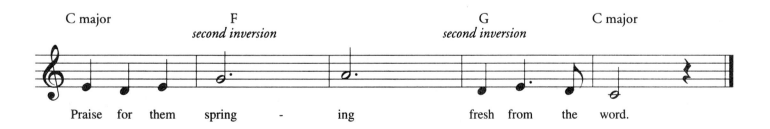

Note that when inverting more complex chords the inversion may actually become a completely different chord.

Altered Triads

When a chord consists of a root, major third, and a perfect fifth it is known as a *major* triad. When the triad is altered by lowering the major third one halfstep, it becomes a *minor* triad. The examples below are chords that have altered intervals.

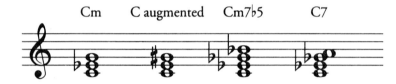

Enharmonic Spelling

Enharmonic tones are tones that have different notation or spelling, but have the same pitch; like C♯ and D♭. You will encounter these differences throughout this book, mostly as altered triads. The reason that this occurs is to make it easier to read while playing from a piece of music manuscript. In the following example, D♭m7♭9 demonstrates why this approach is practical and preferred. As stated before, triads are superposed thirds or notes that are stacked one on top of the other.

This allows the musician to see, at a glance, what chord they are going to play. So with this in mind, look at the D♭m7♭9 example. You will notice that the E♭ is double flatted (E♭♭), this allows the musician, again at a glance, to see that what would be the nine of the chord is now flatted. The other example is indeed the same chord, but by using the D instead of the E♭♭ the chord becomes harder to read.

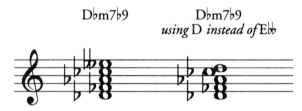

Progressions

The chord progression of a piece of music is its harmonic framework. As you become familiar with different types of music you will find various forms of progressions. One of the most popular and widely used is the I-IV-V, which was derived from early blues styles. I, IV, and V are the first, fourth, and fifth steps of a scale. The following examples are in the key of C, so the chords that would correspond to this progression are C major, F major, and G major.

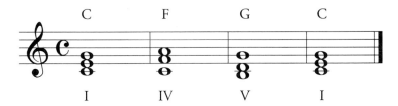

Here are some bass lines to use with the I-IV-V.

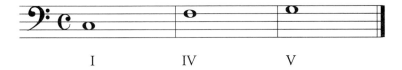

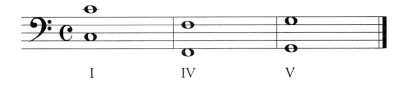

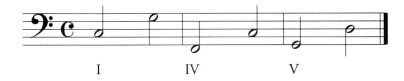

I   IV   V

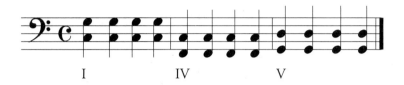

I   IV   V

Try these other familiar progressions.

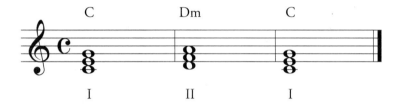

I   II   I

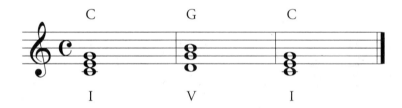

I   V   I

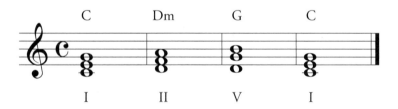

I   II   V   I

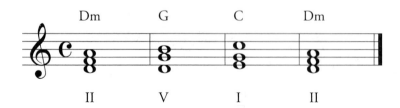

II   V   I   II

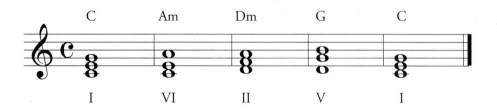

I   VI   II   V   I